Doodle Art

COLORING BOOKS FOR ADULTS

Vol.2

Animal and Variety Mandala Design

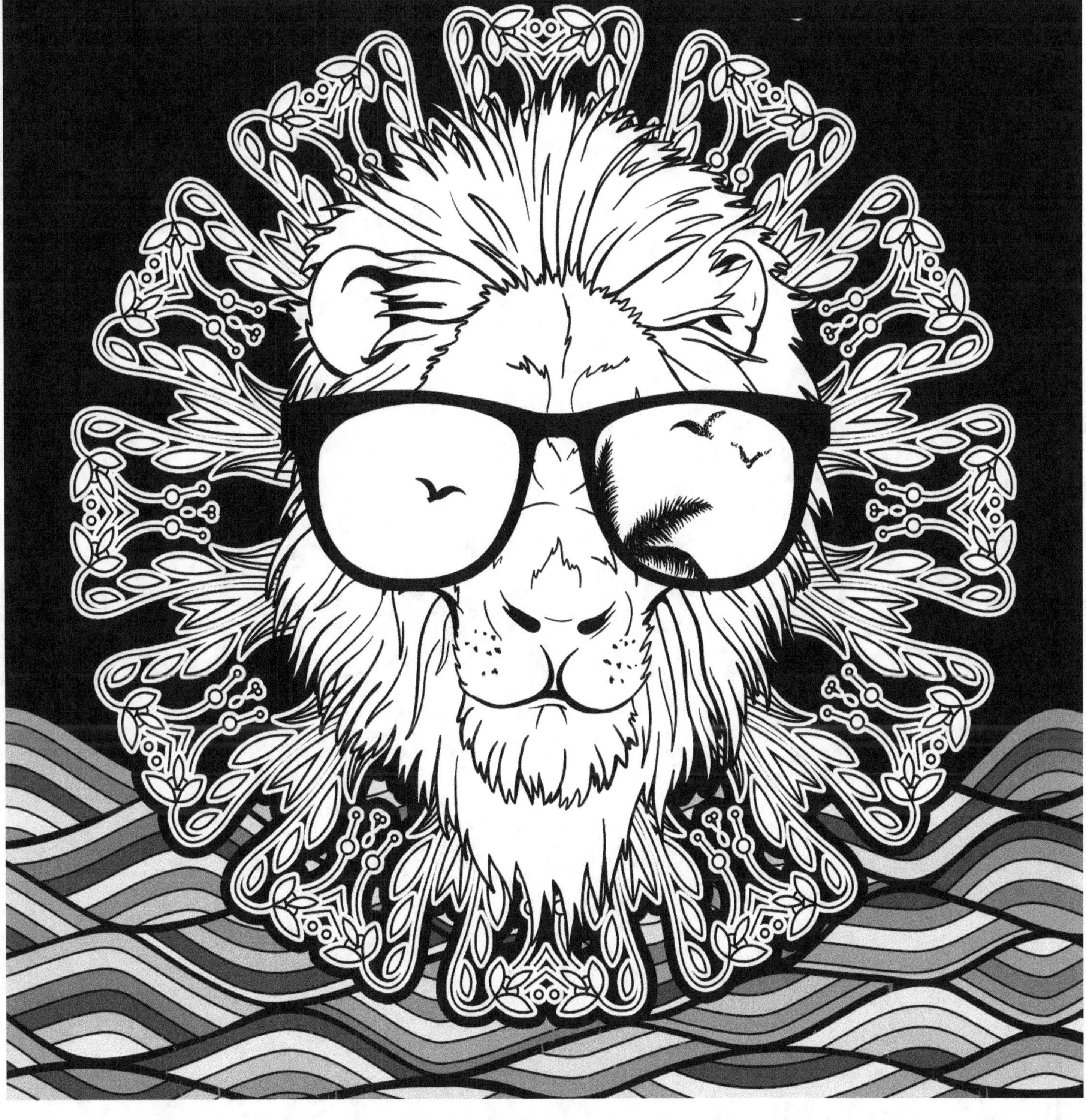

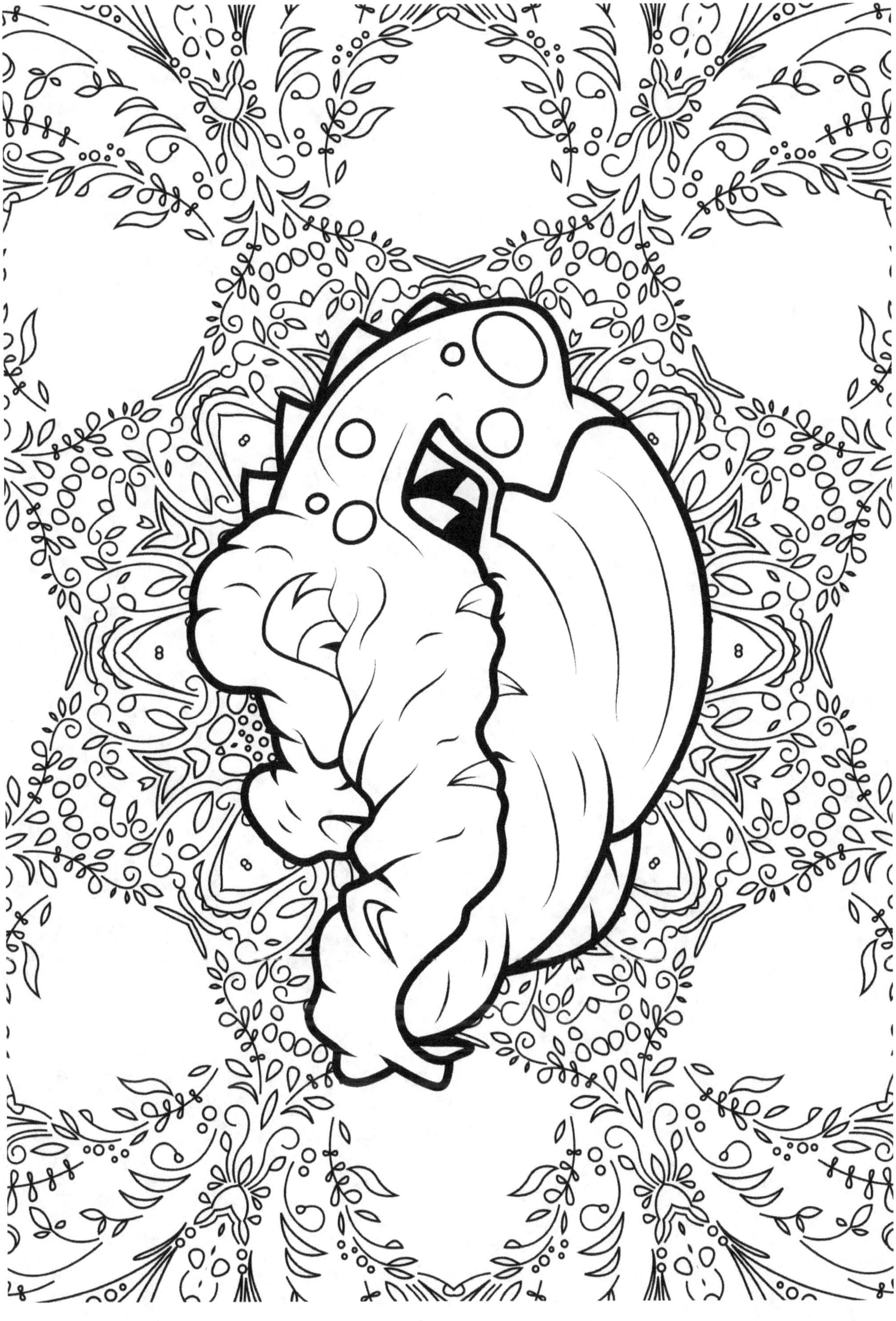

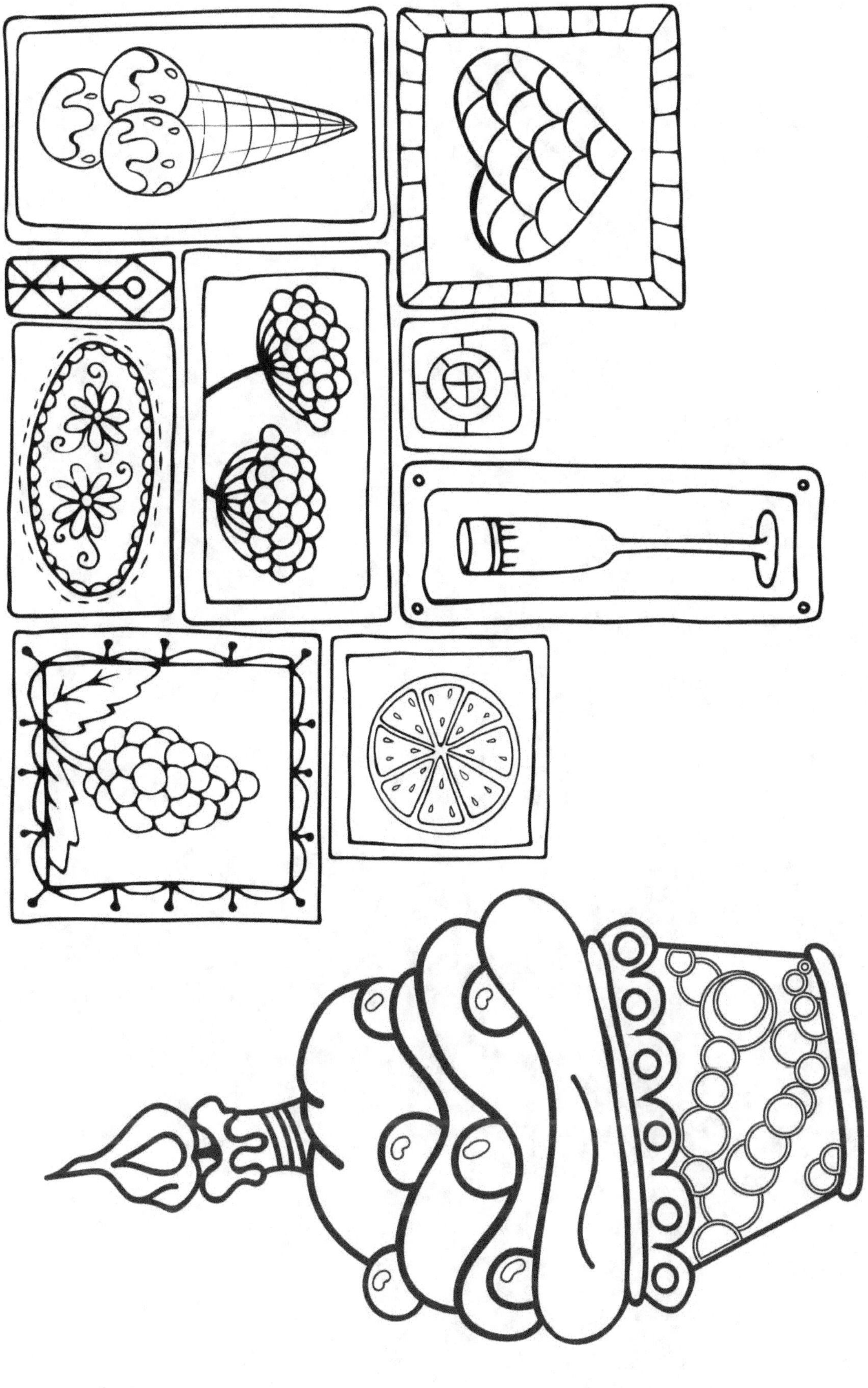

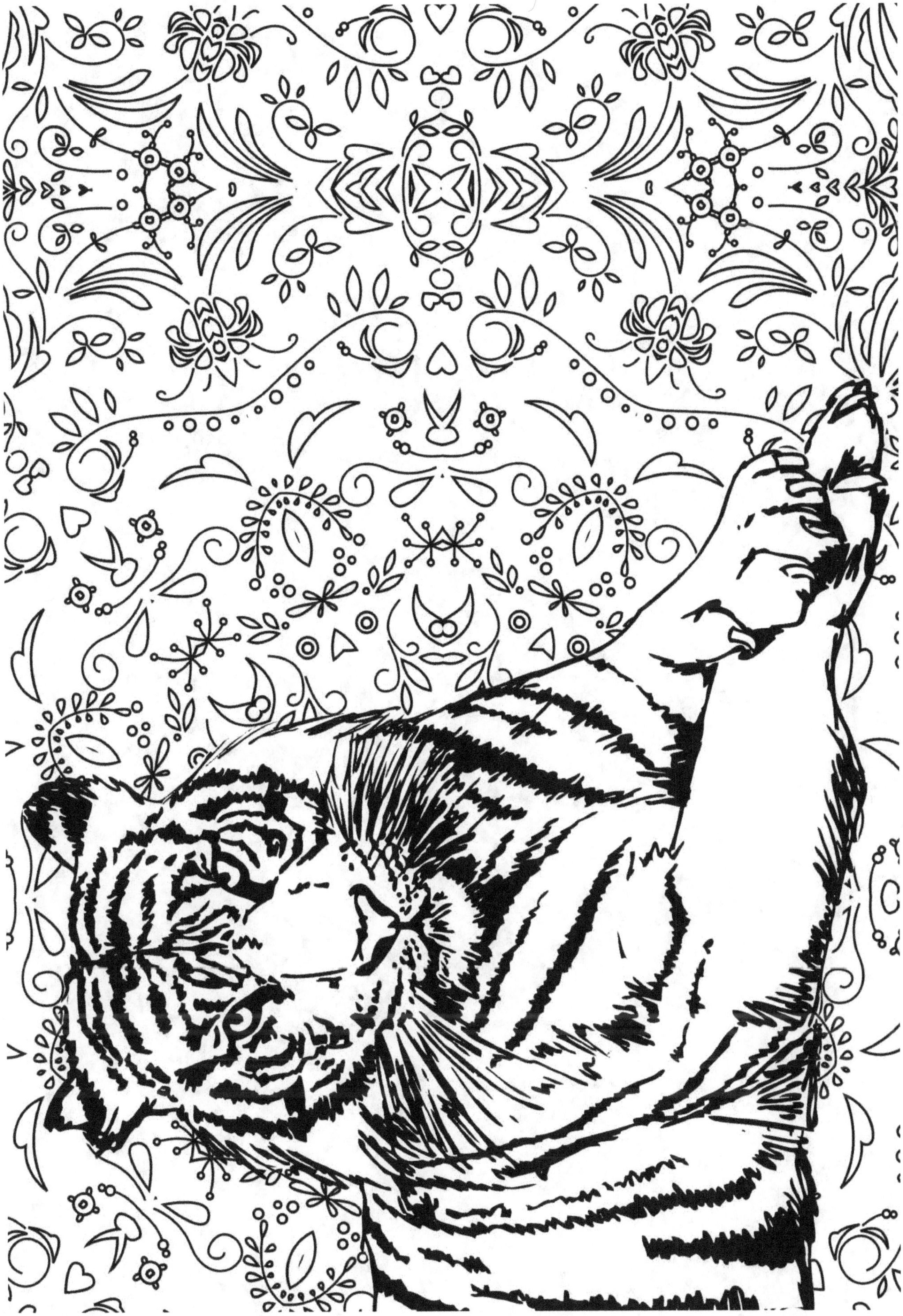

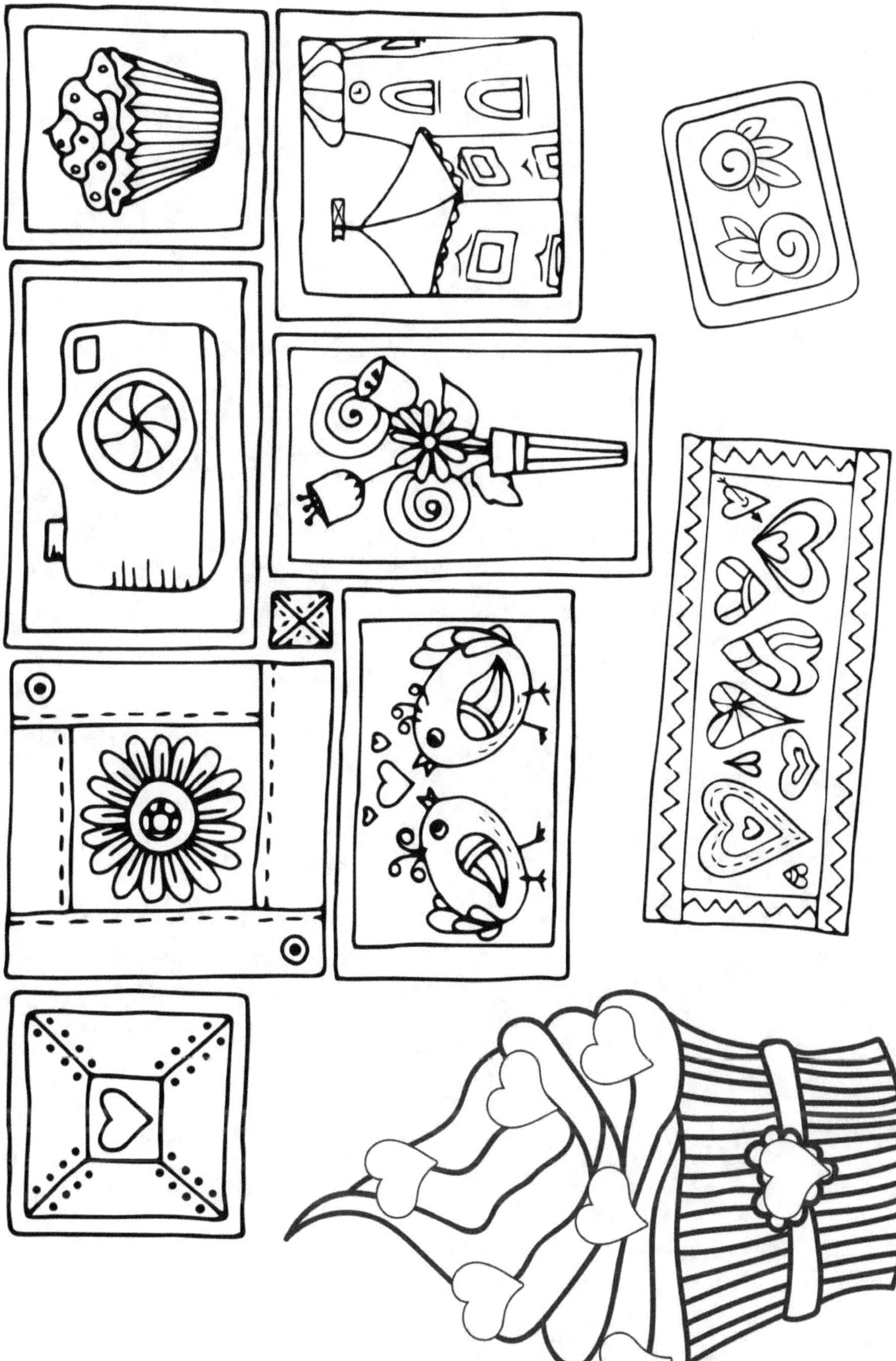

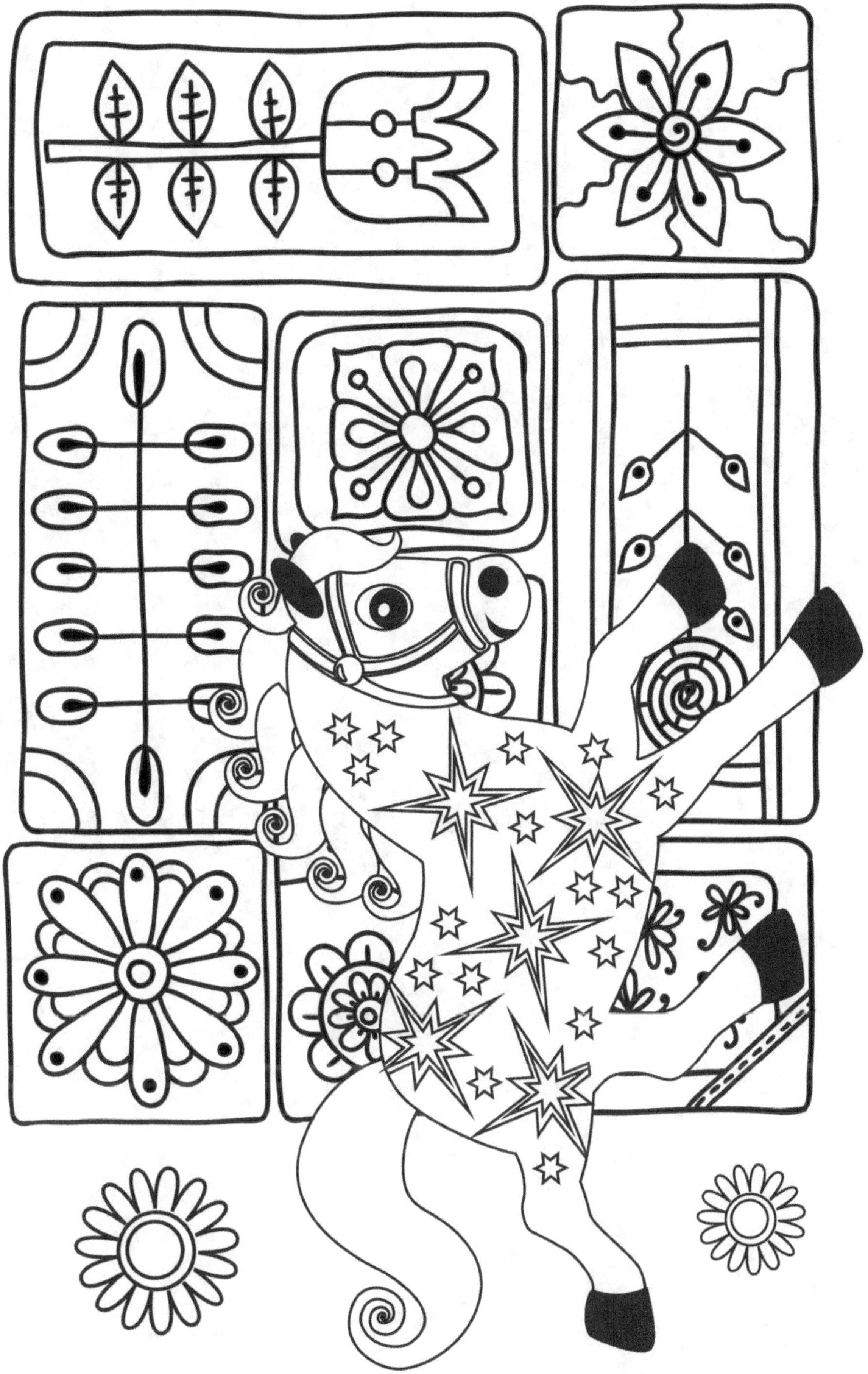

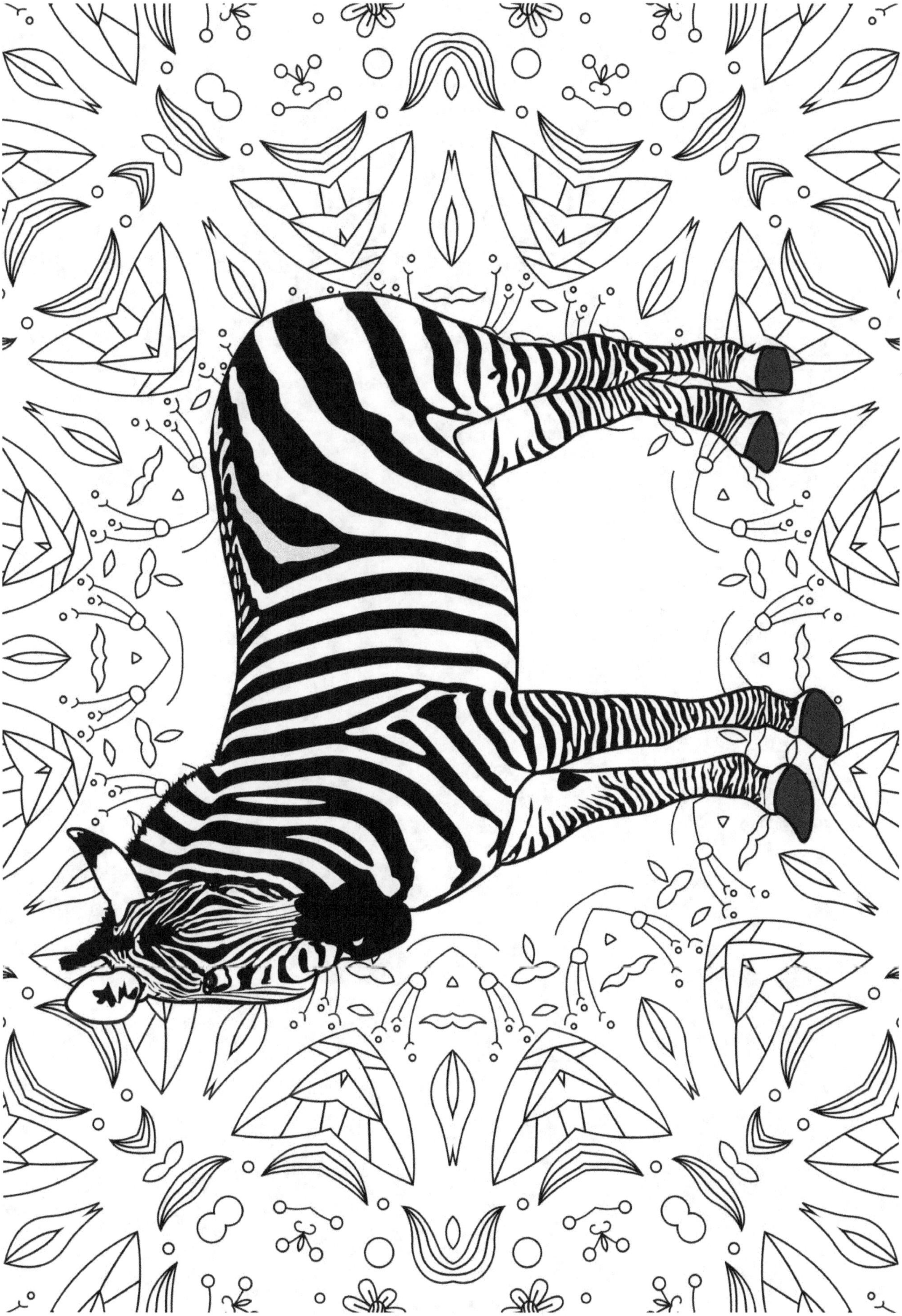

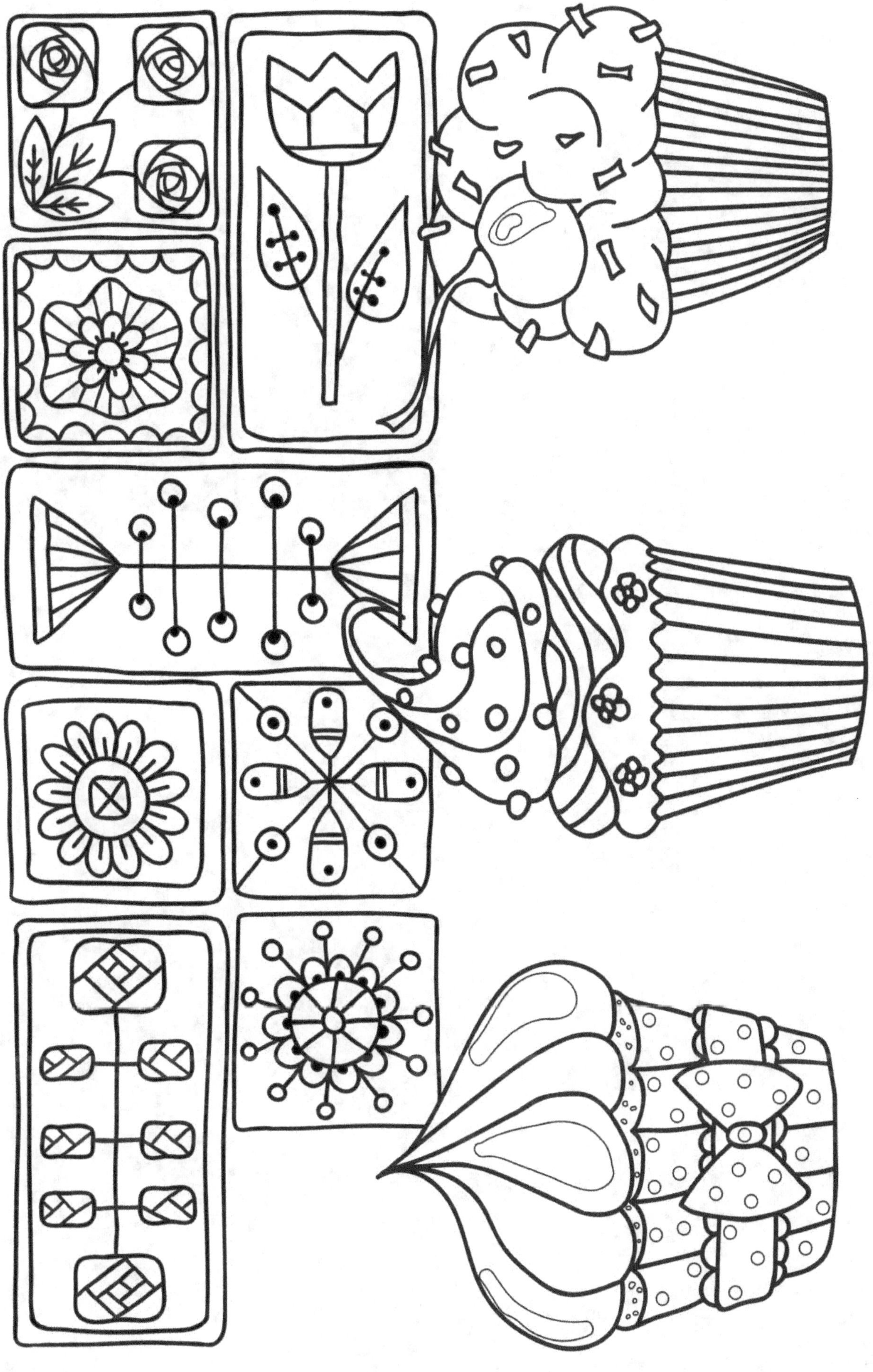

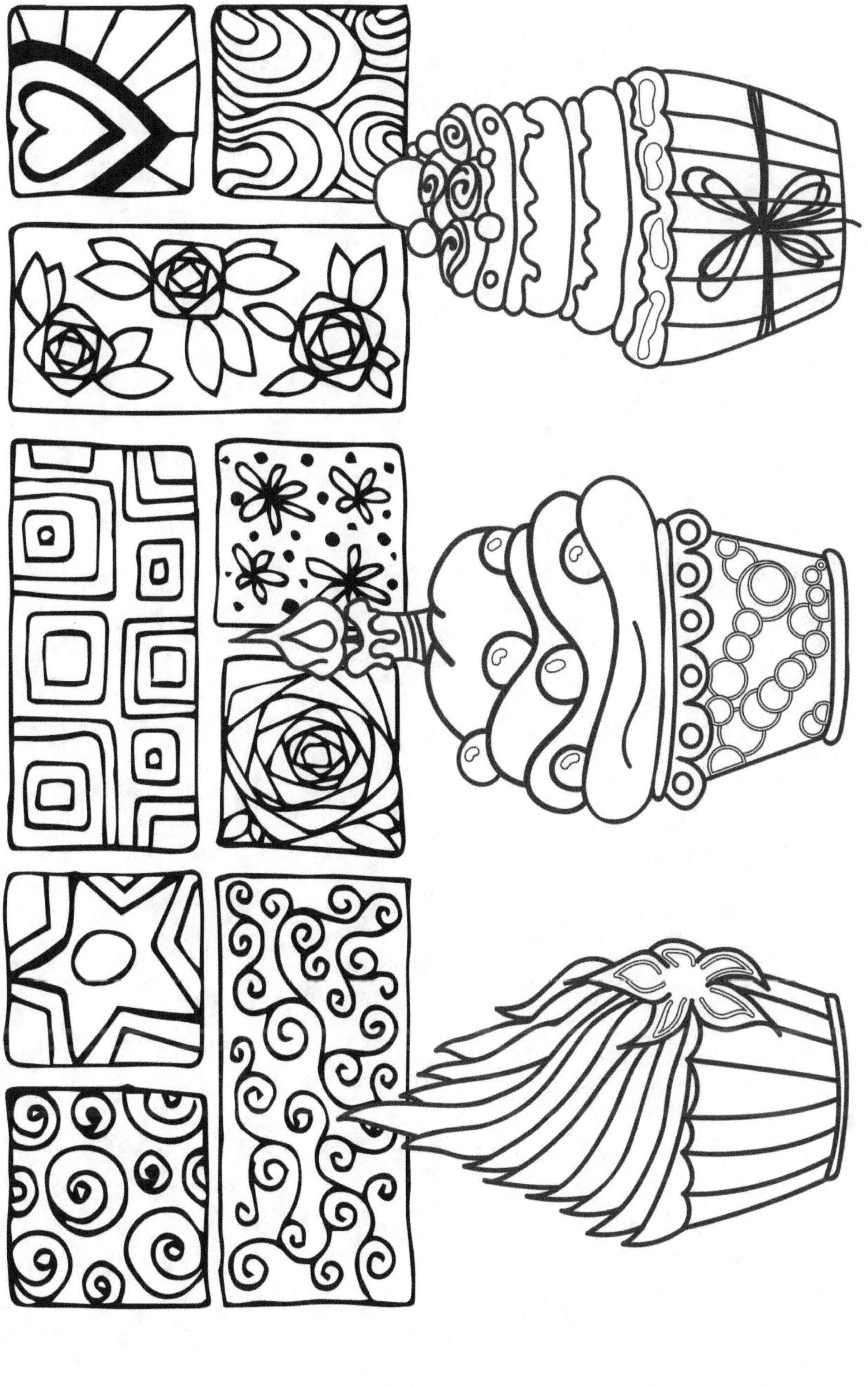

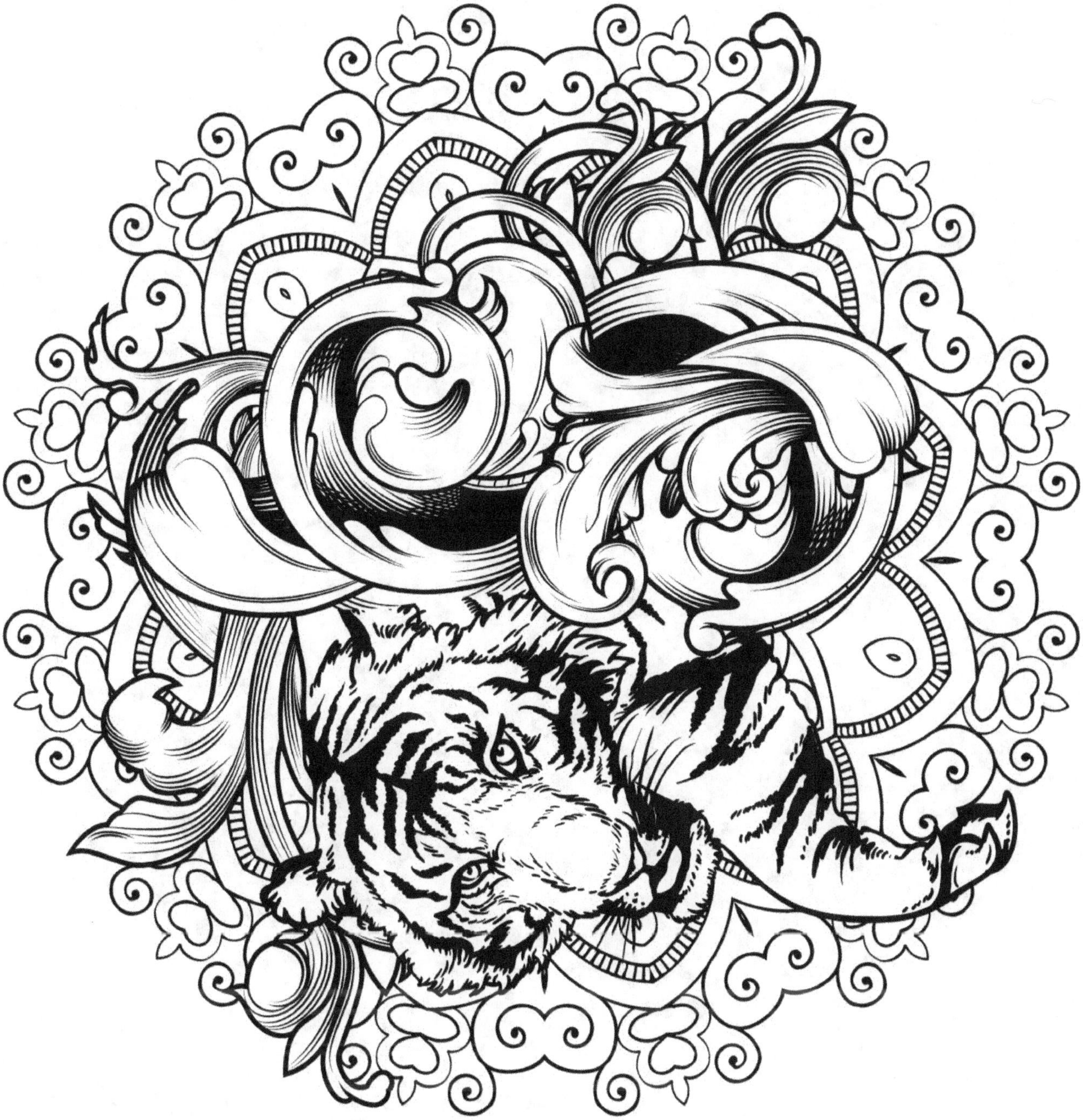

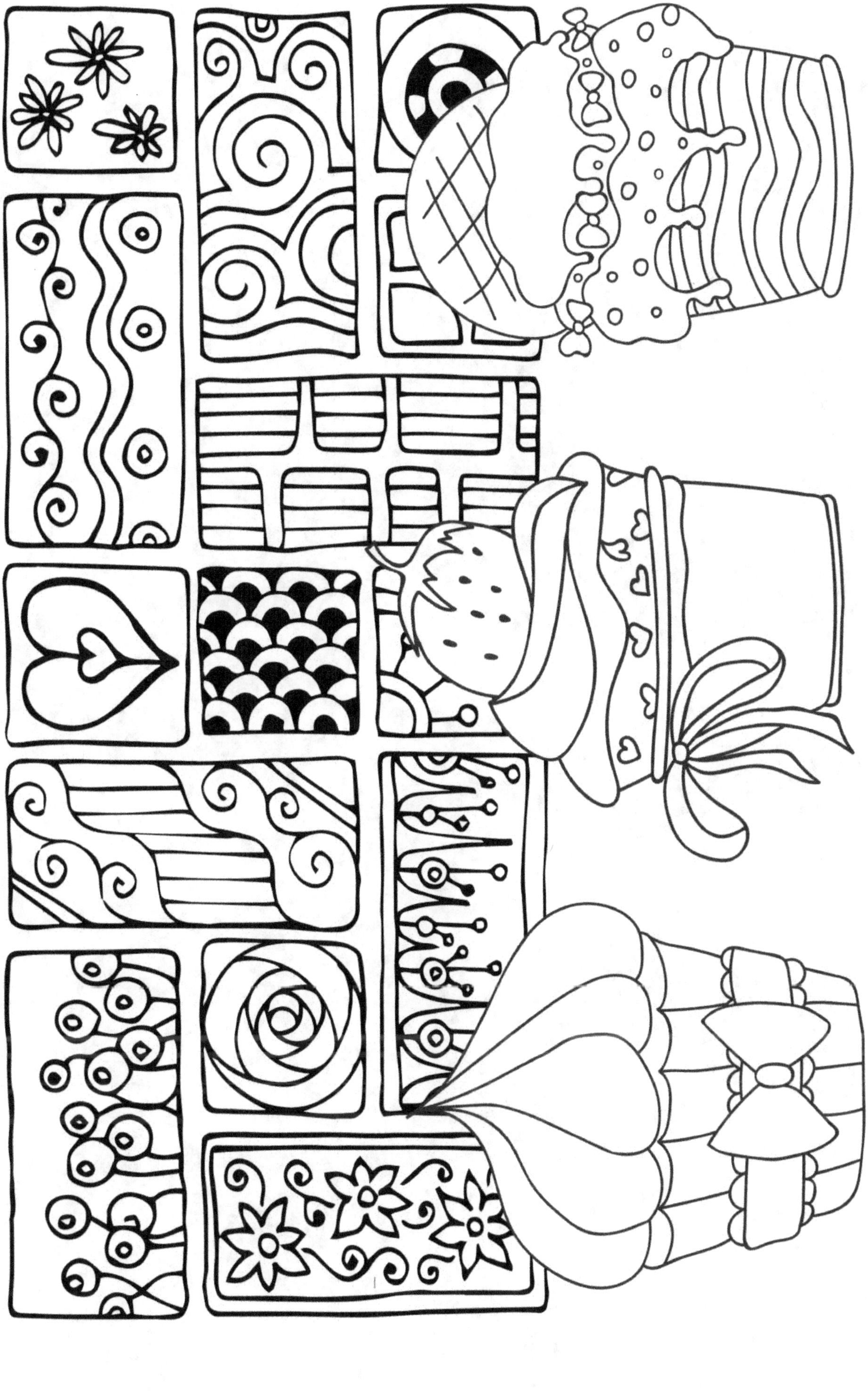

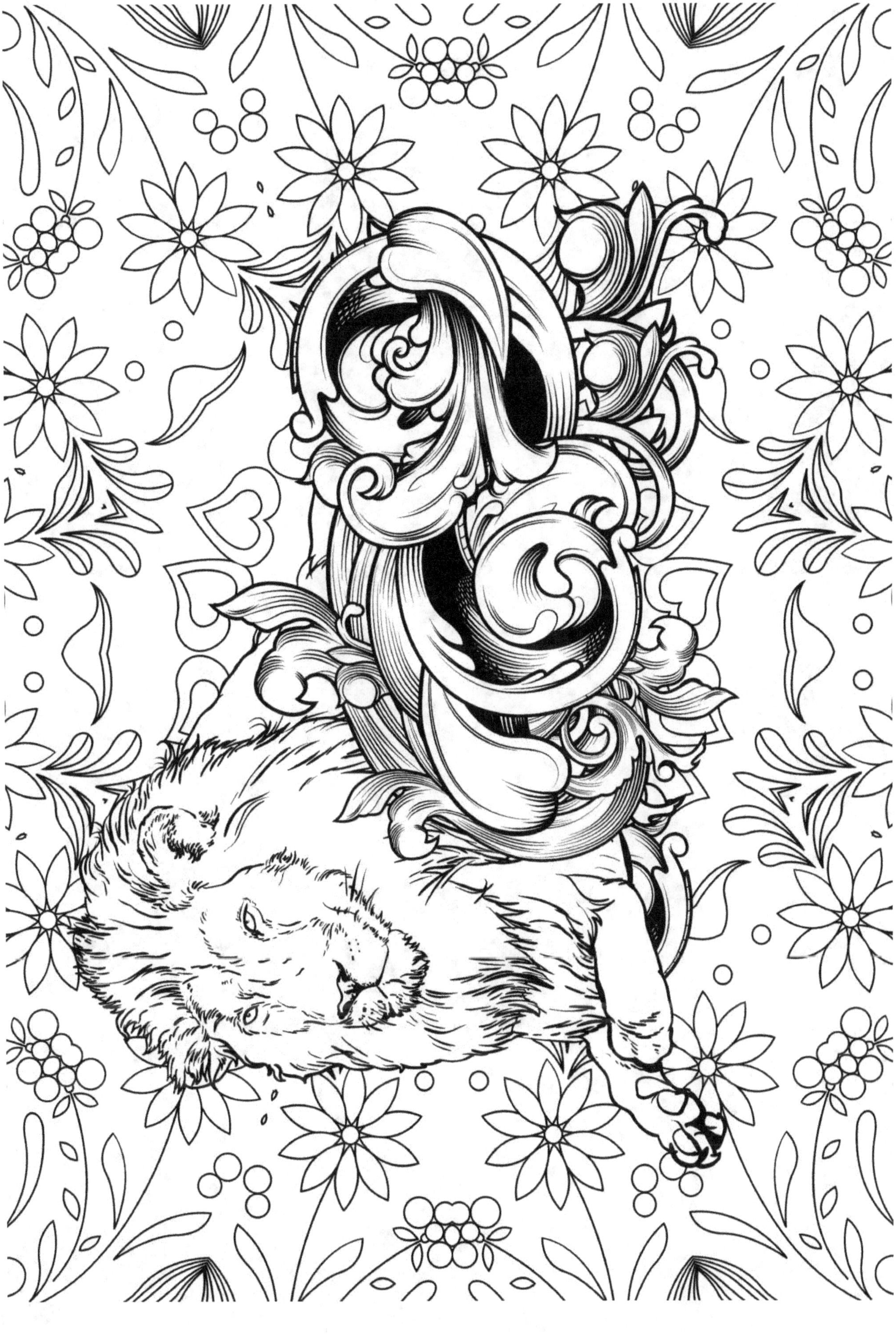

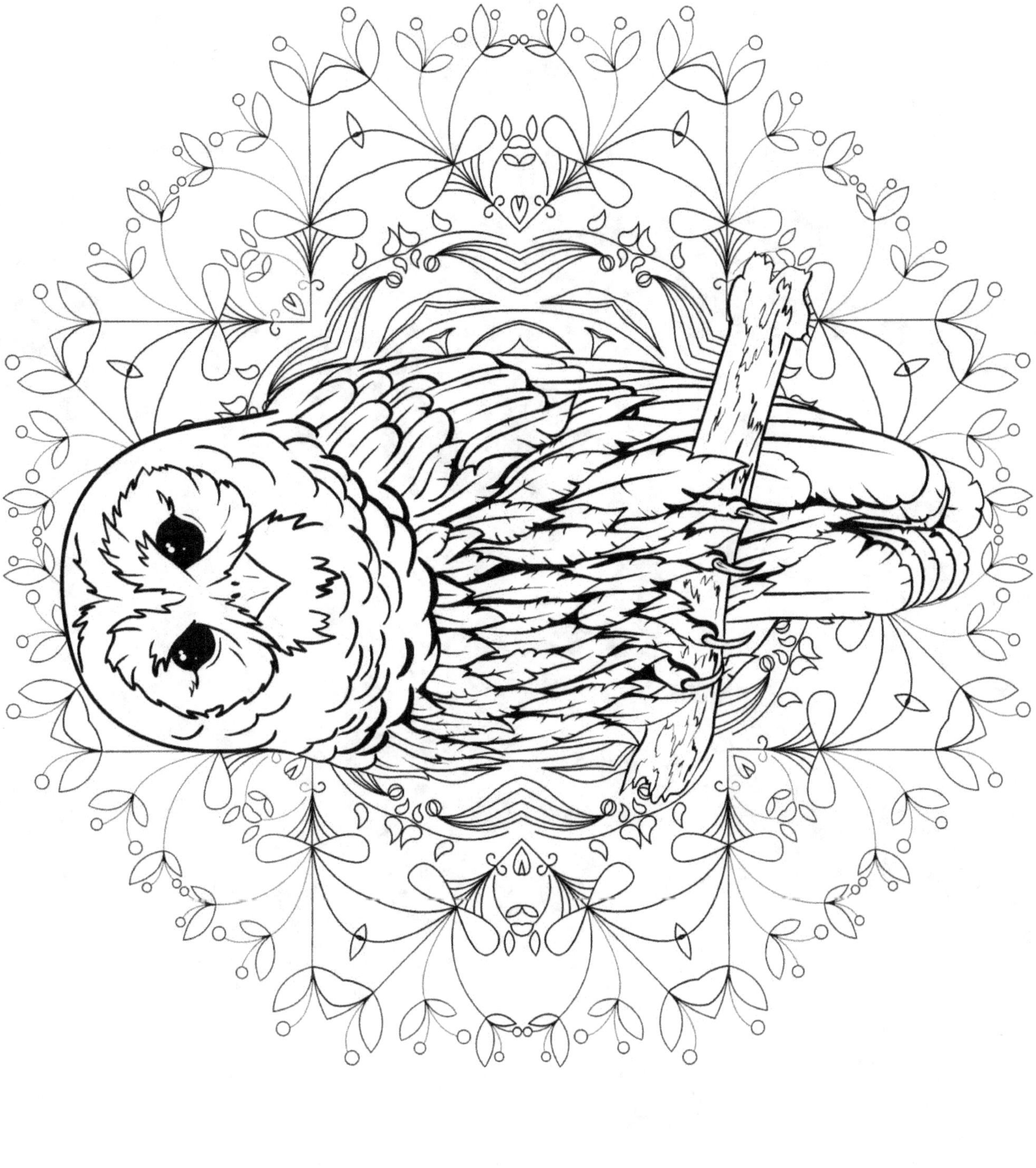

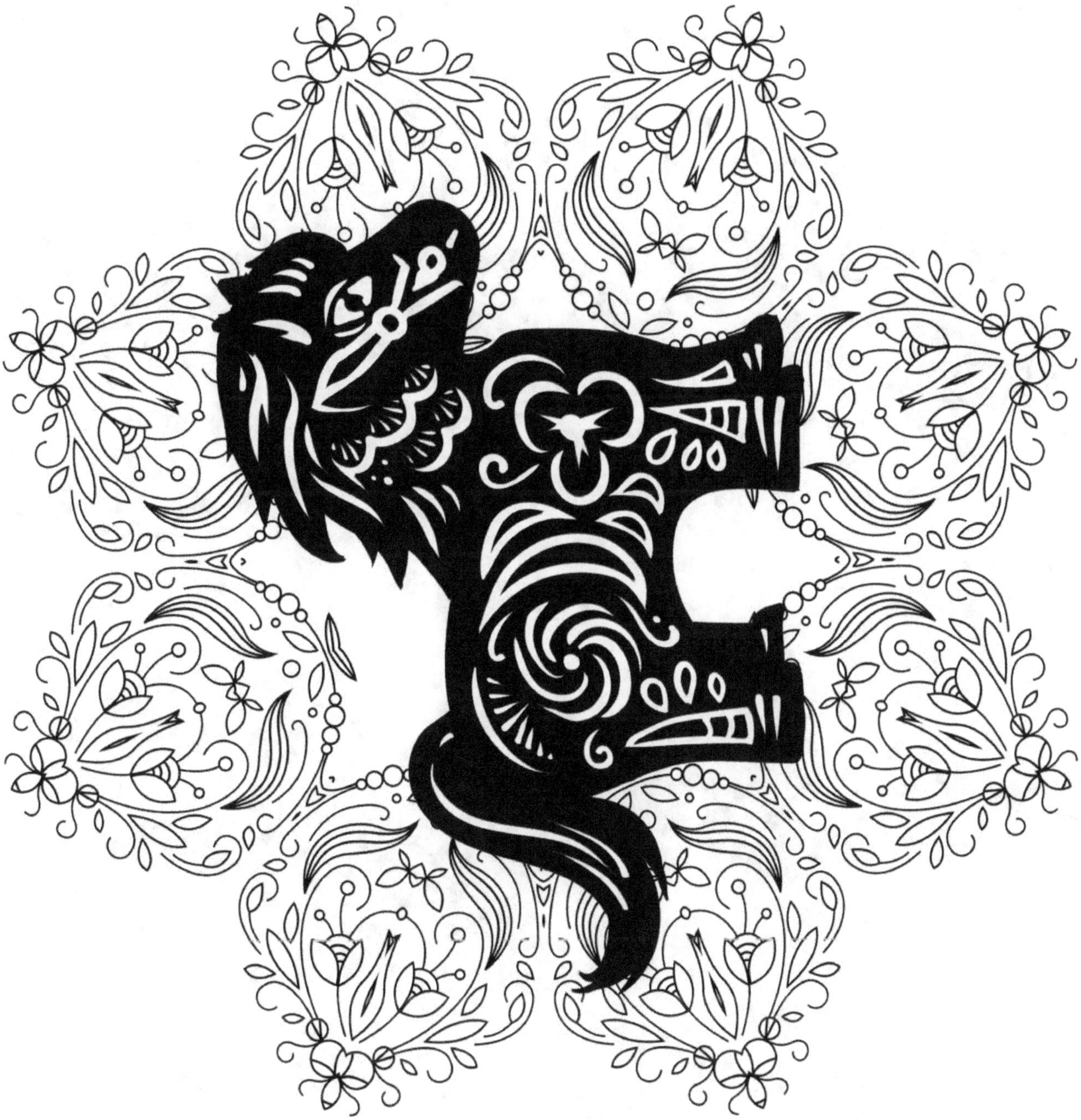

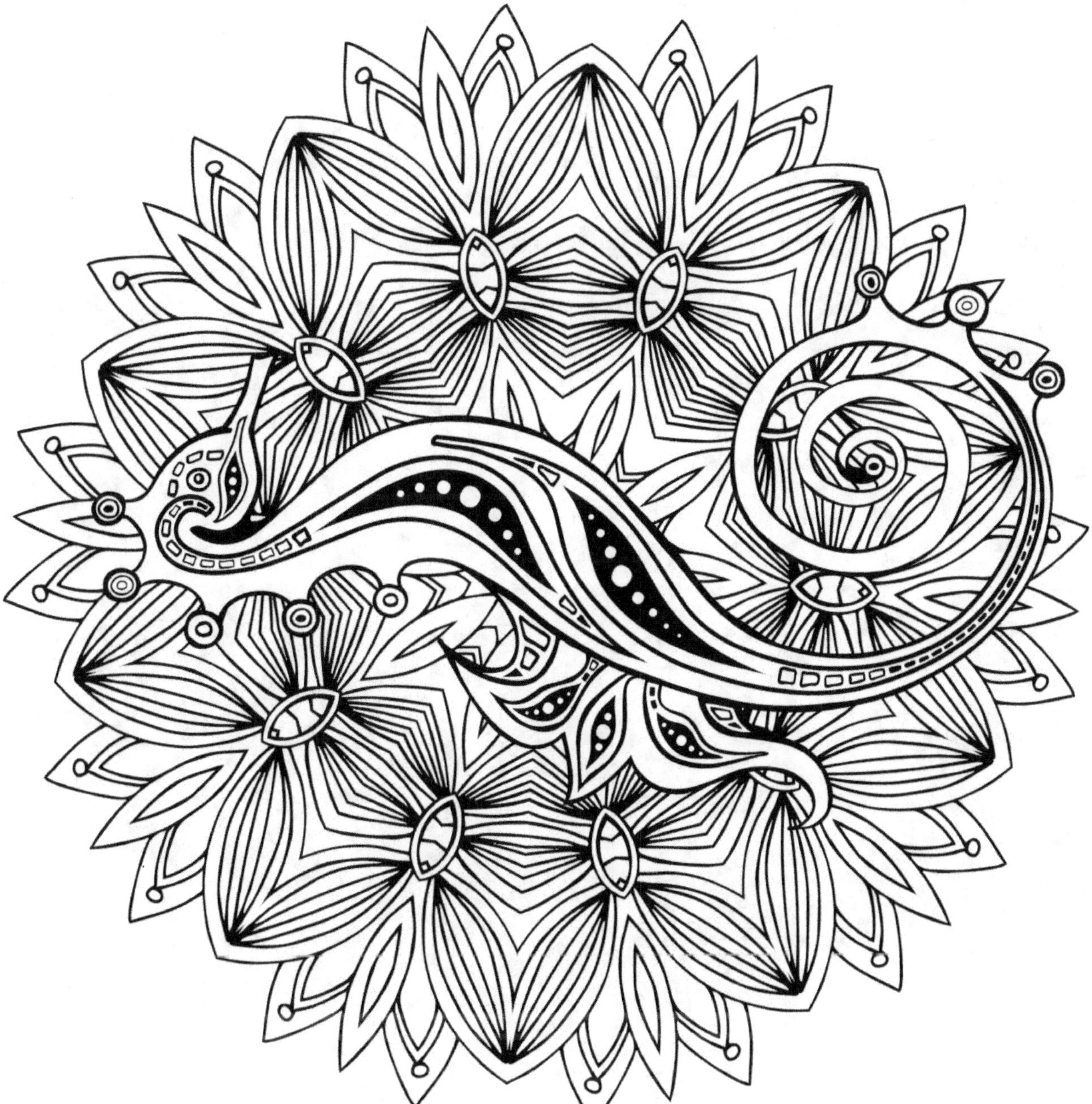

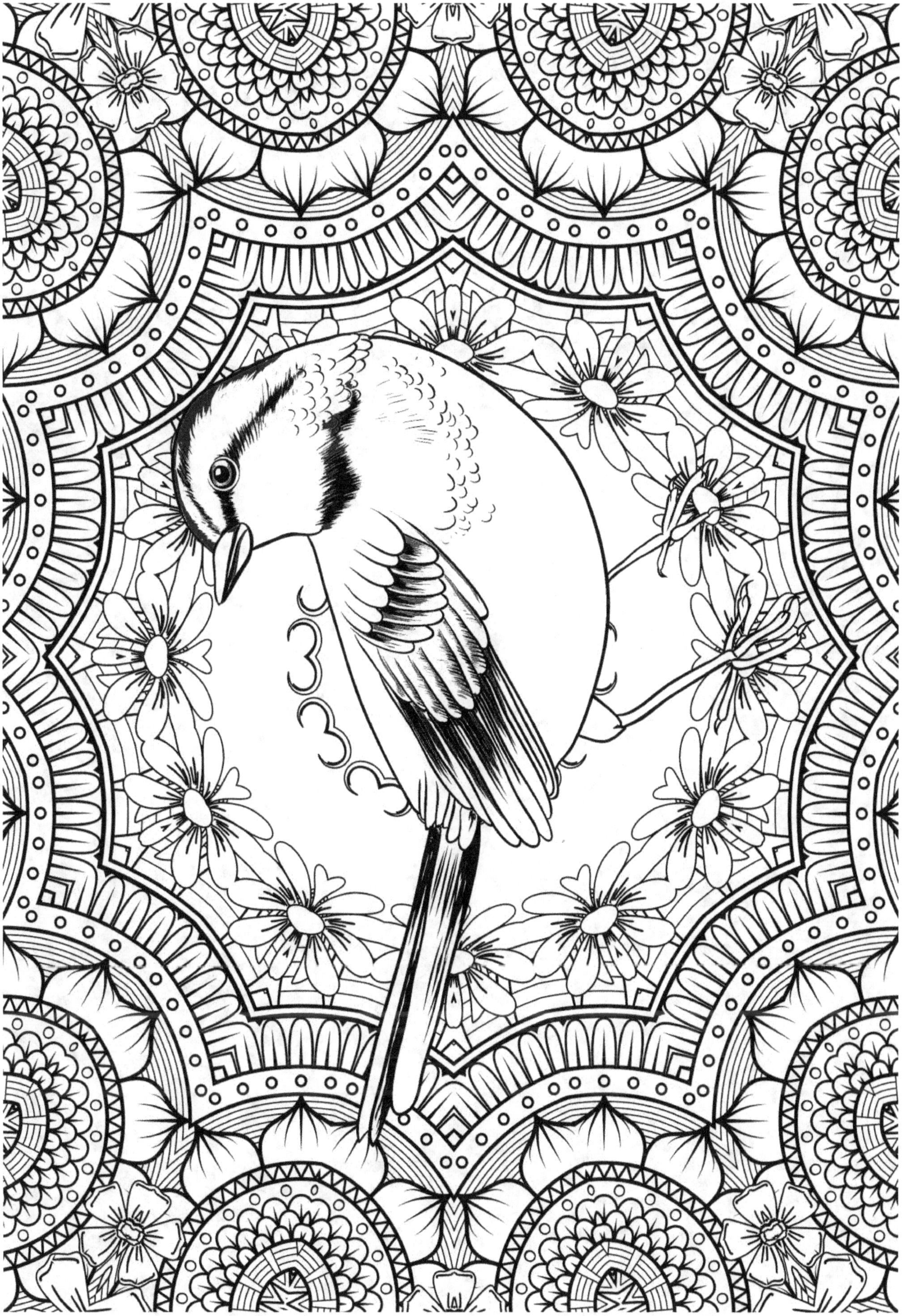

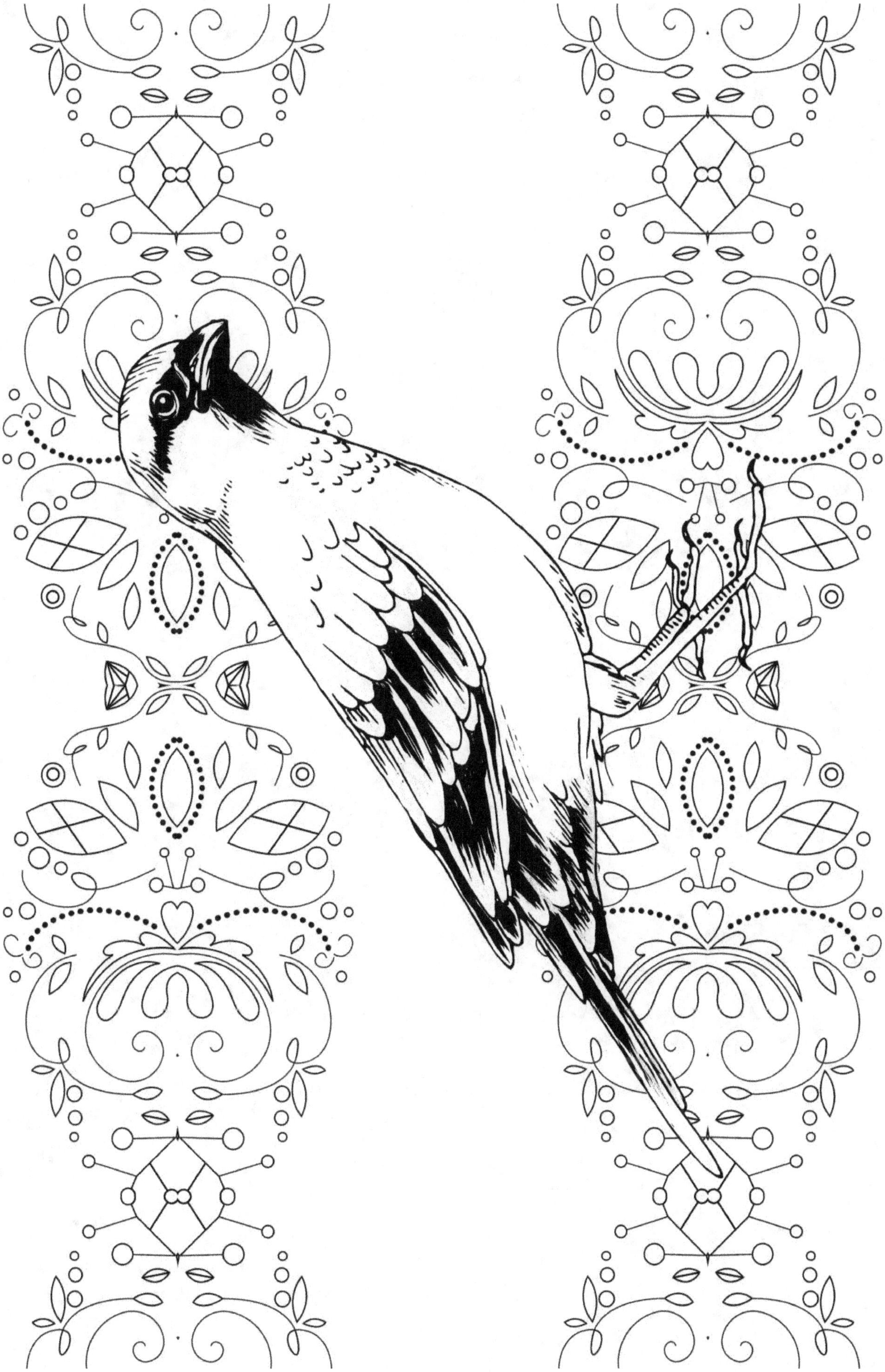

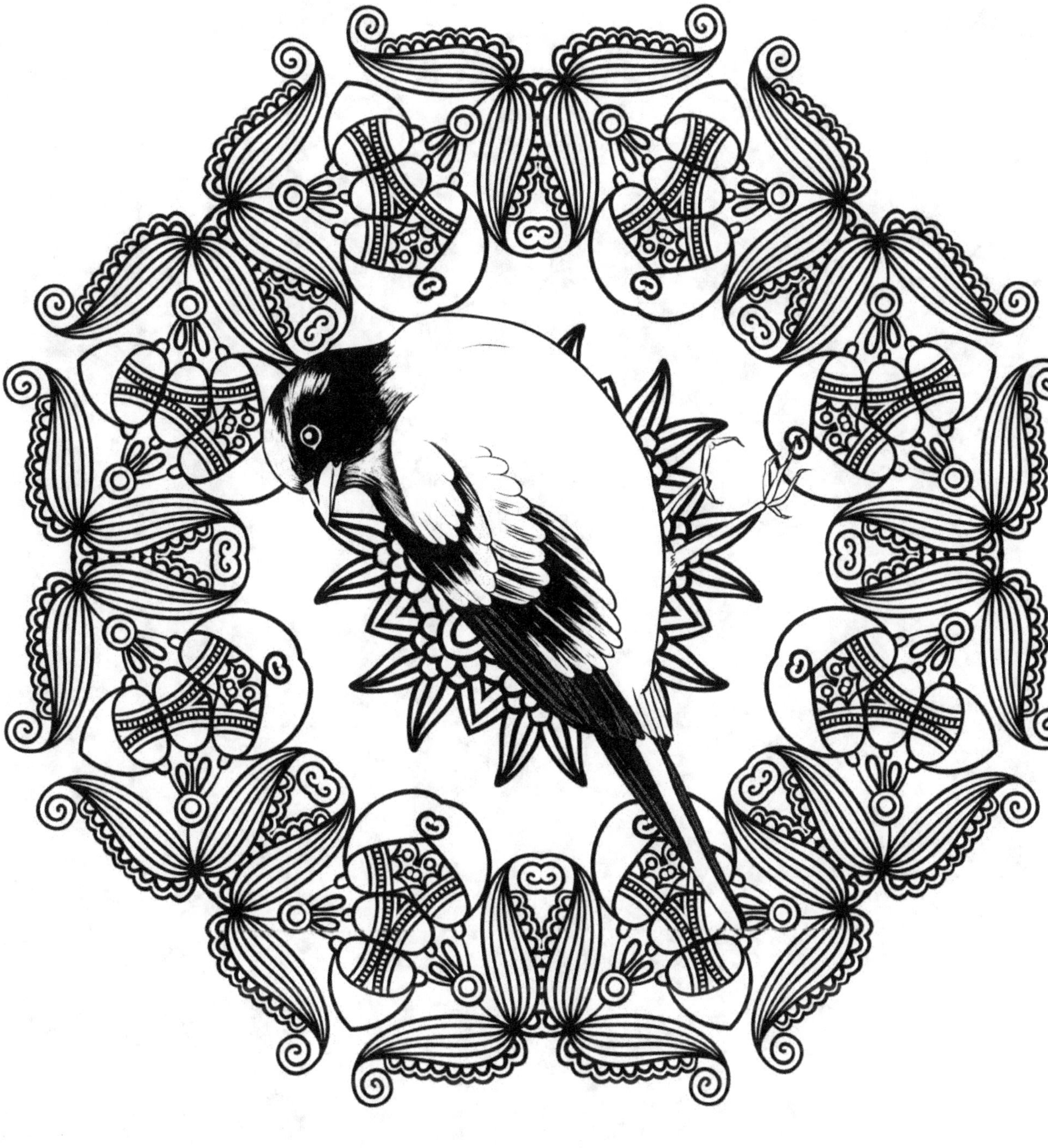

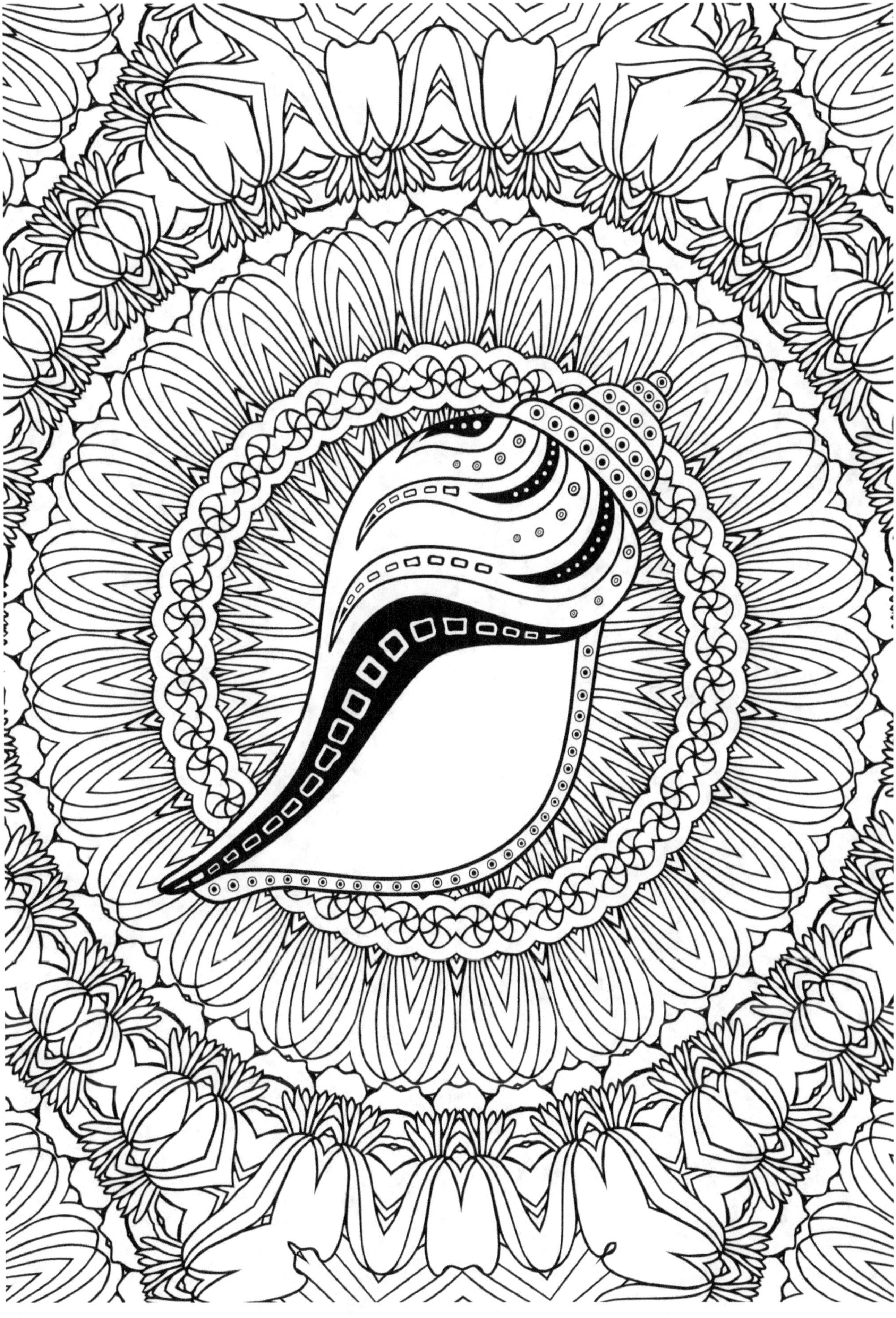

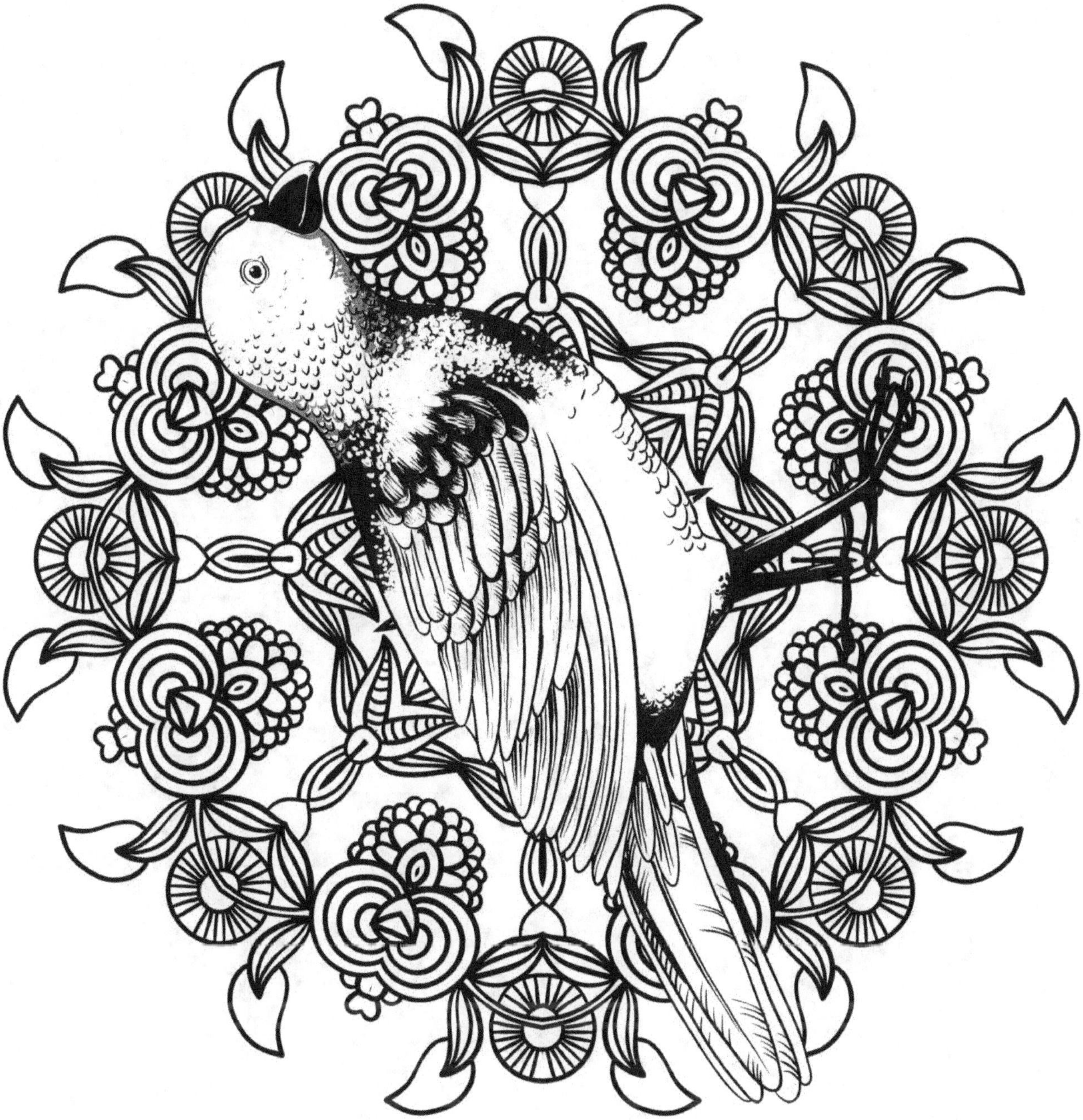

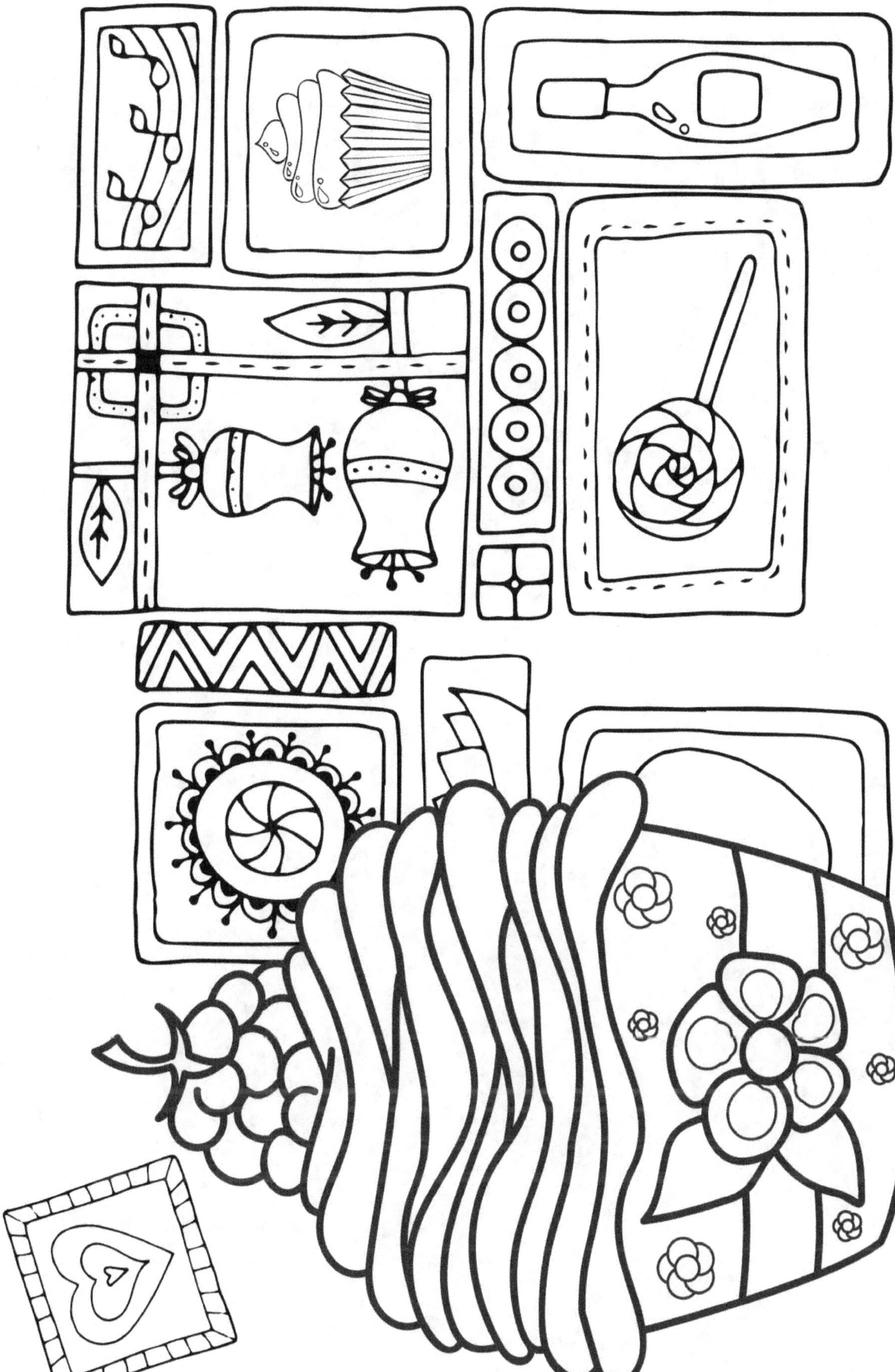

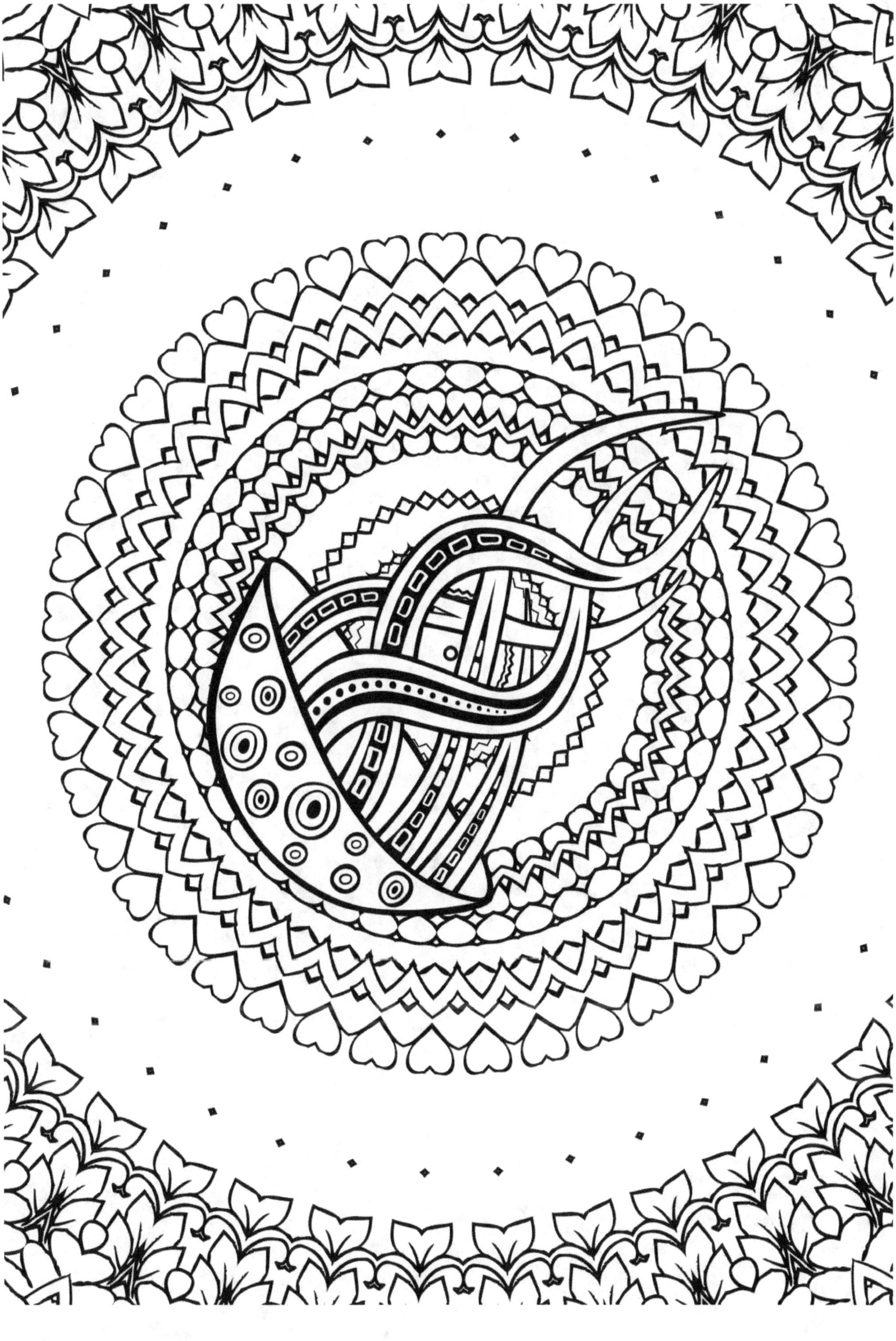

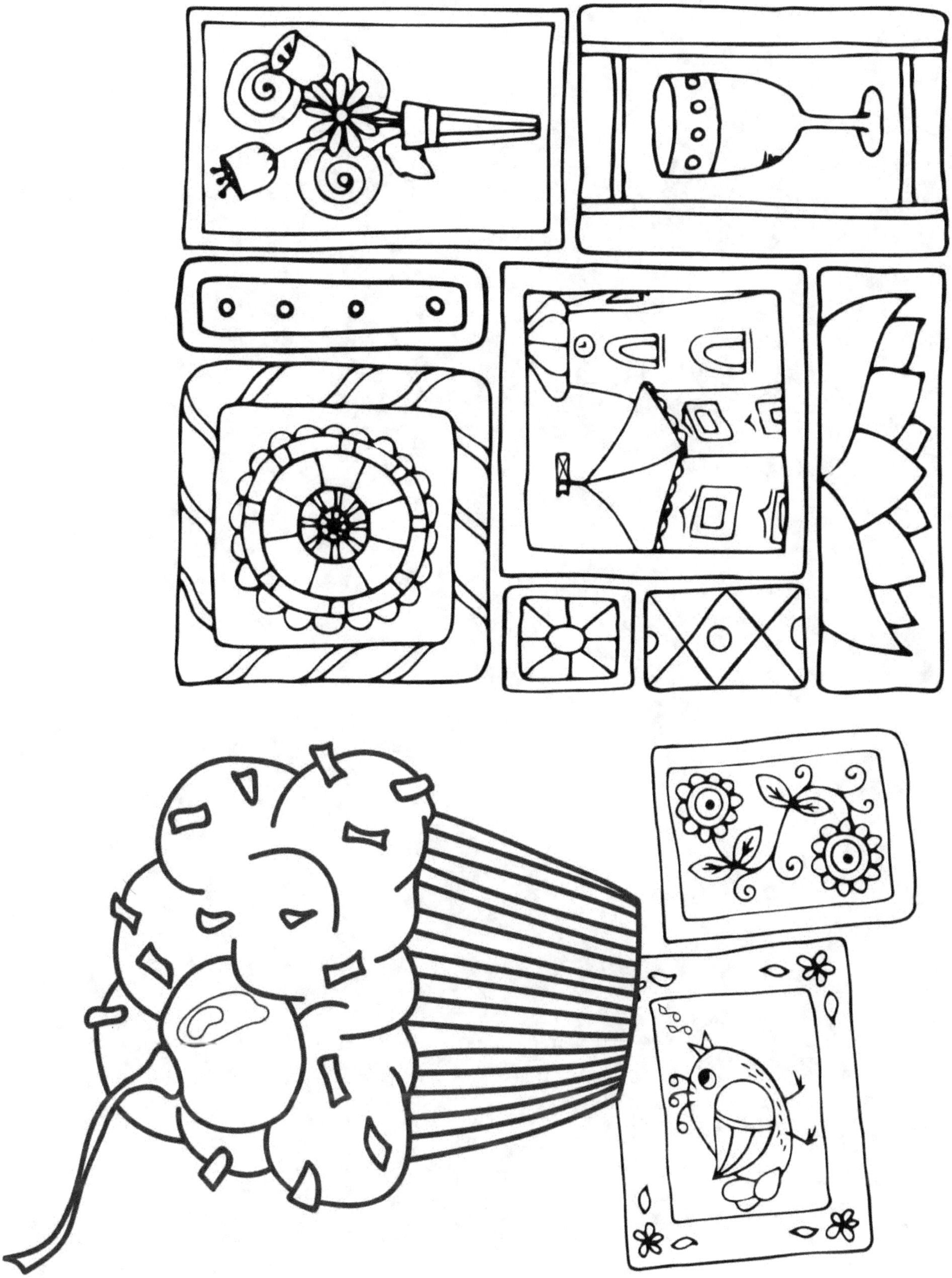

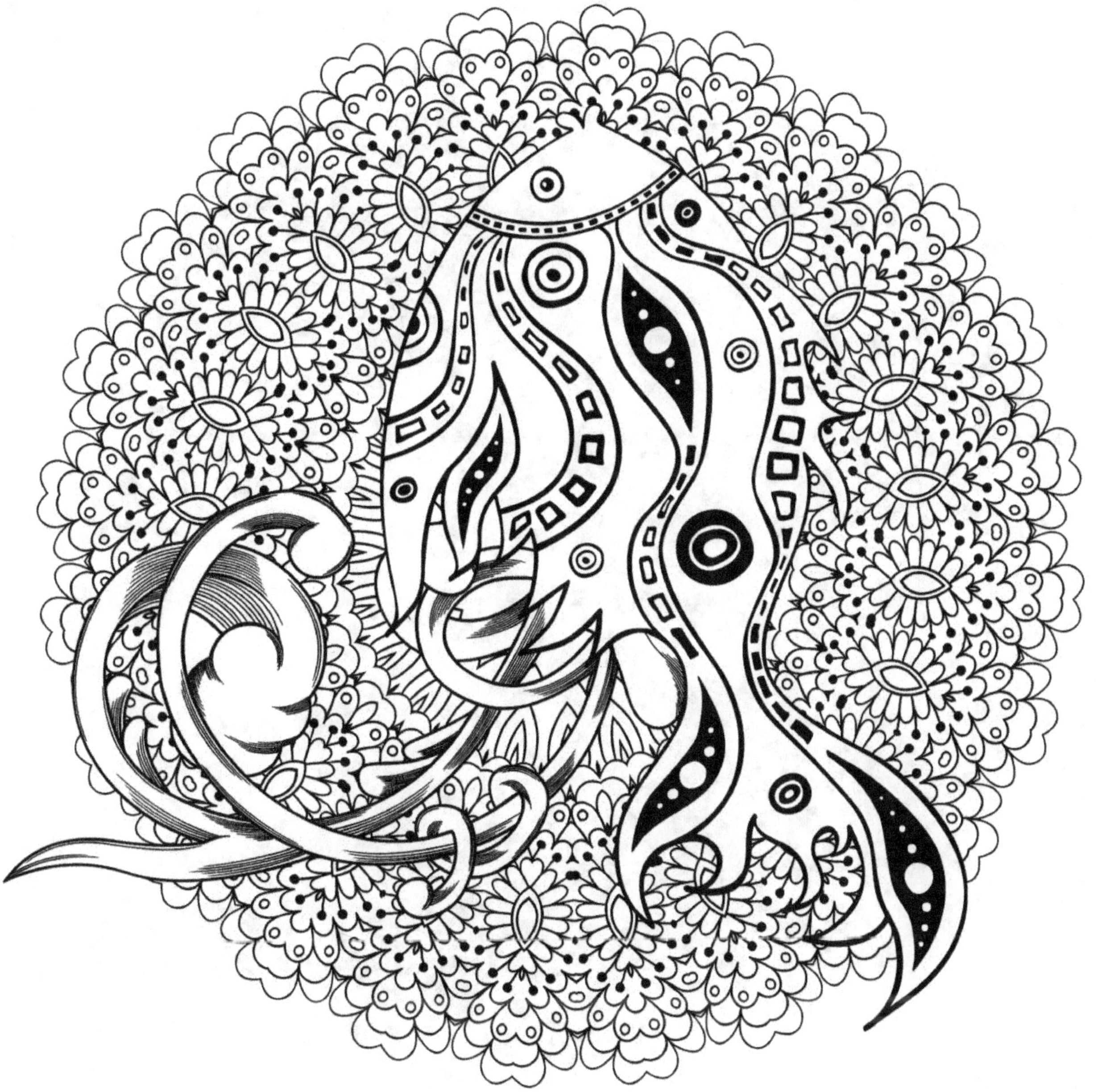

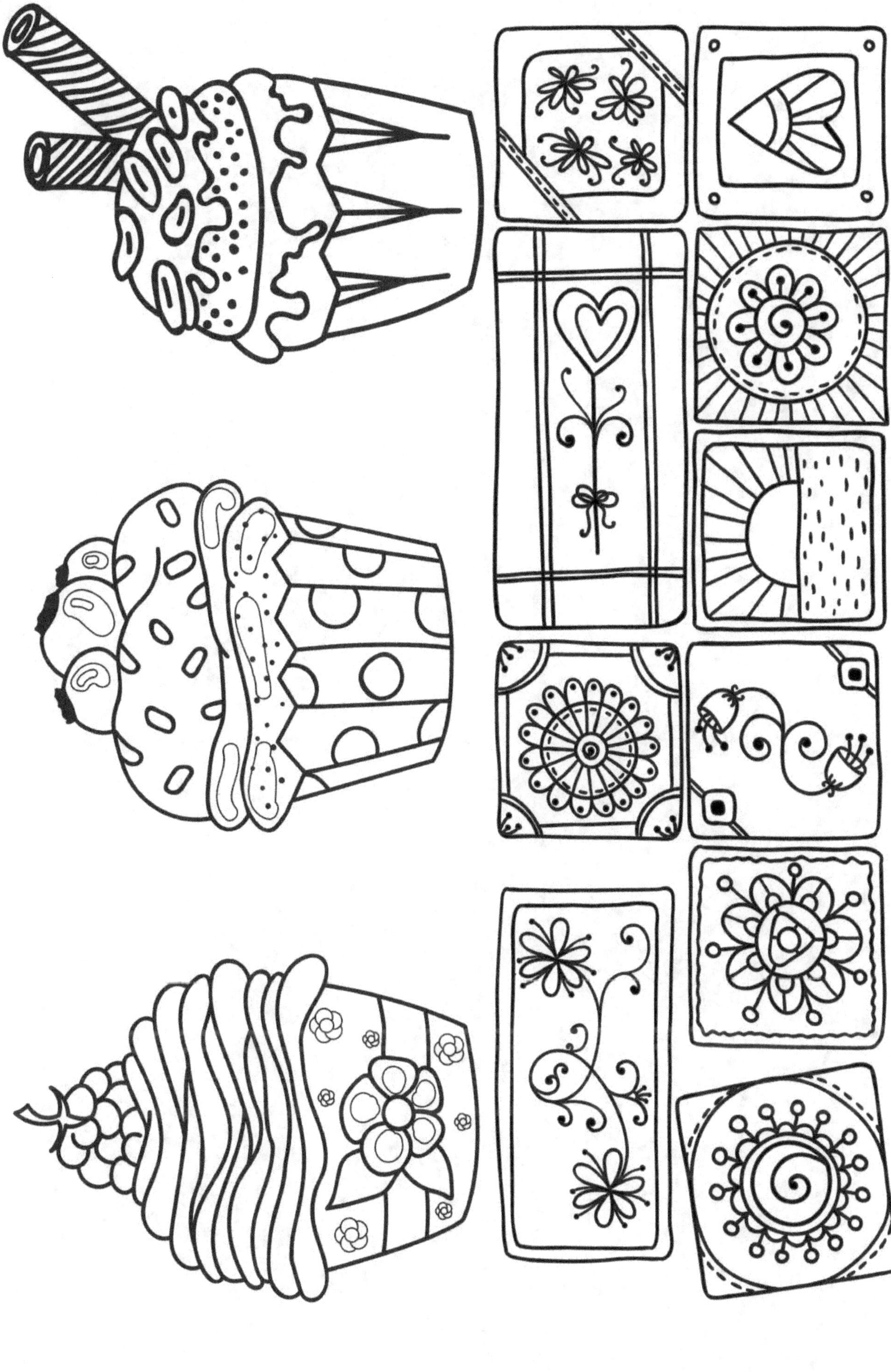

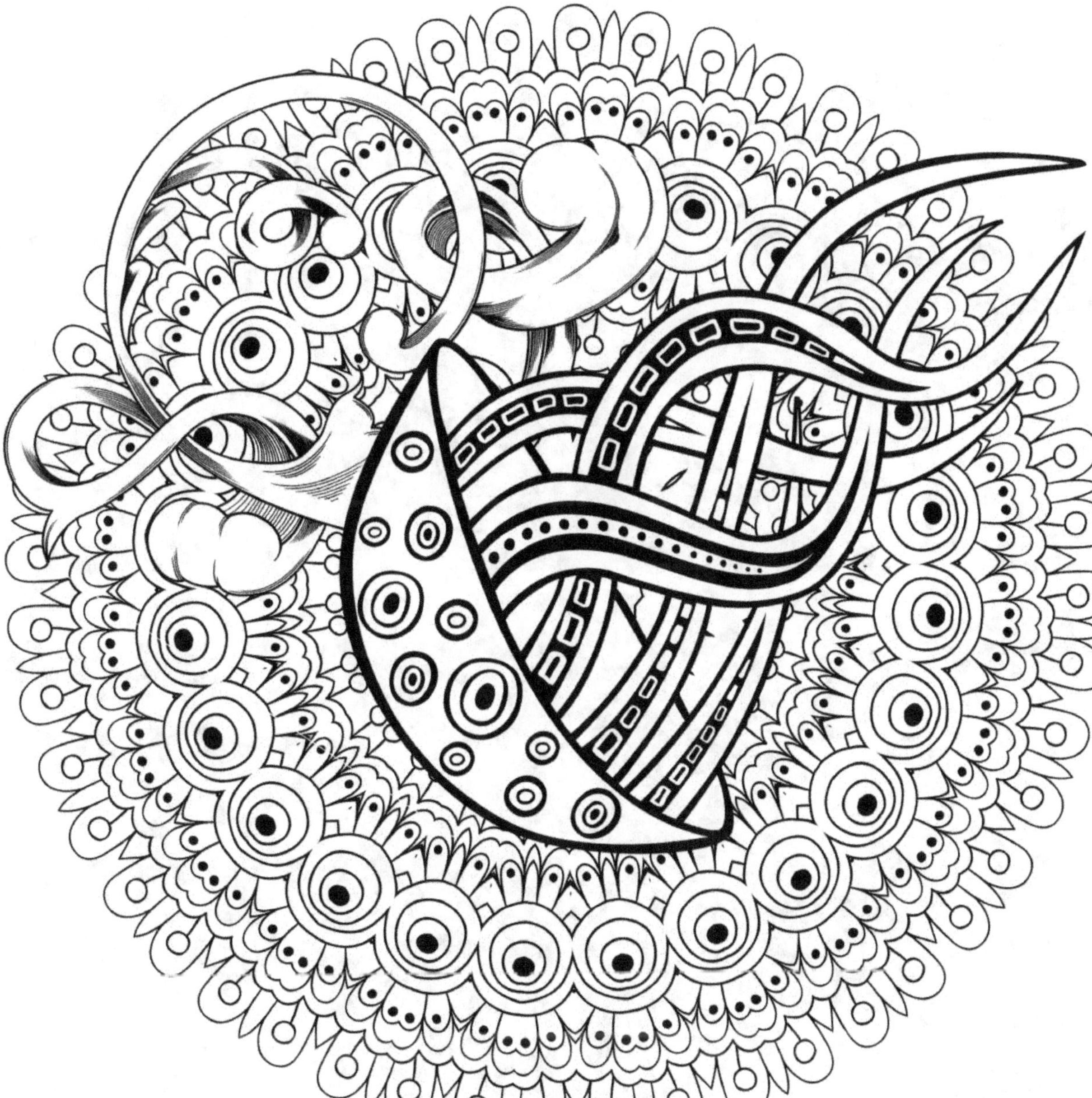

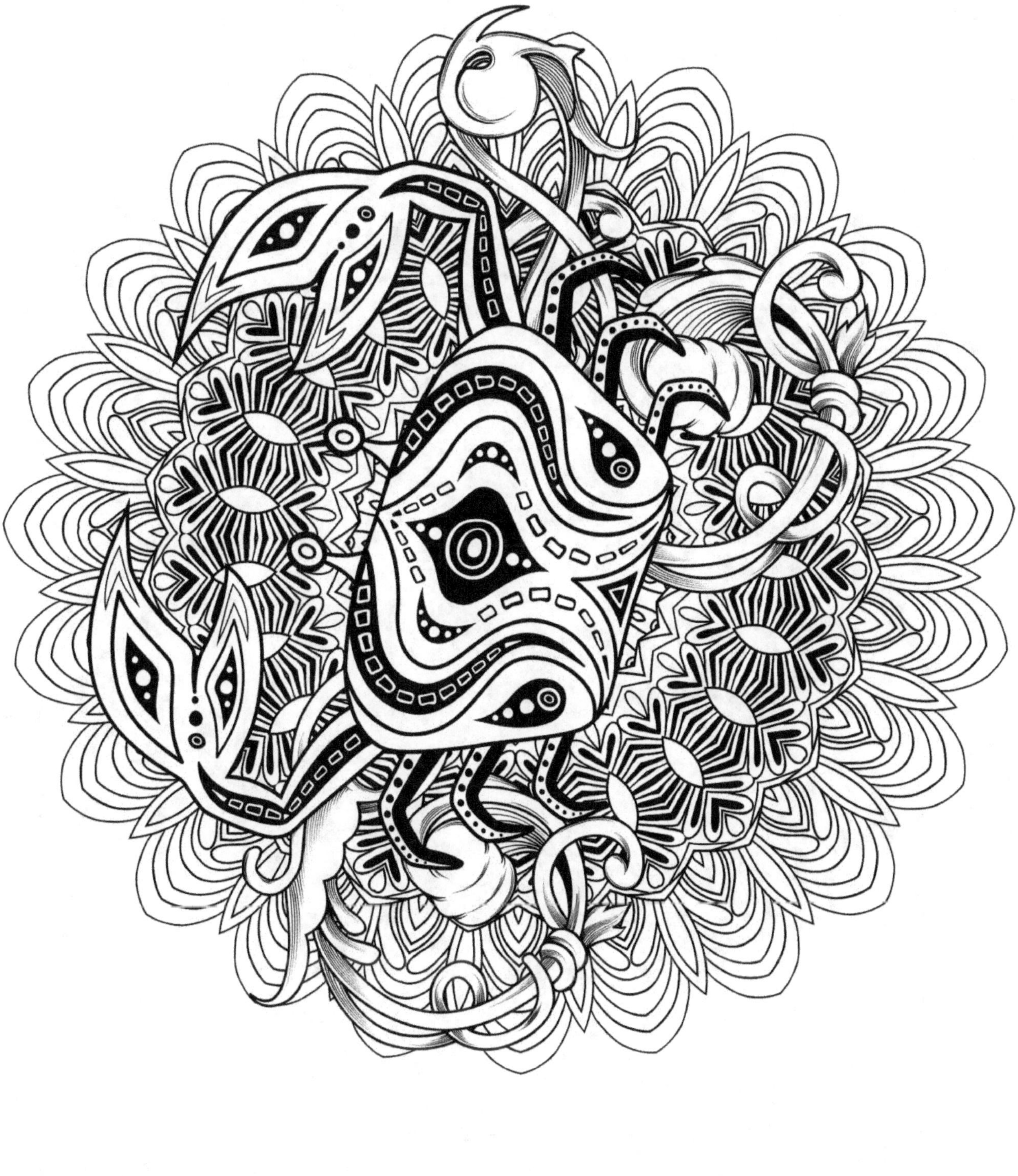

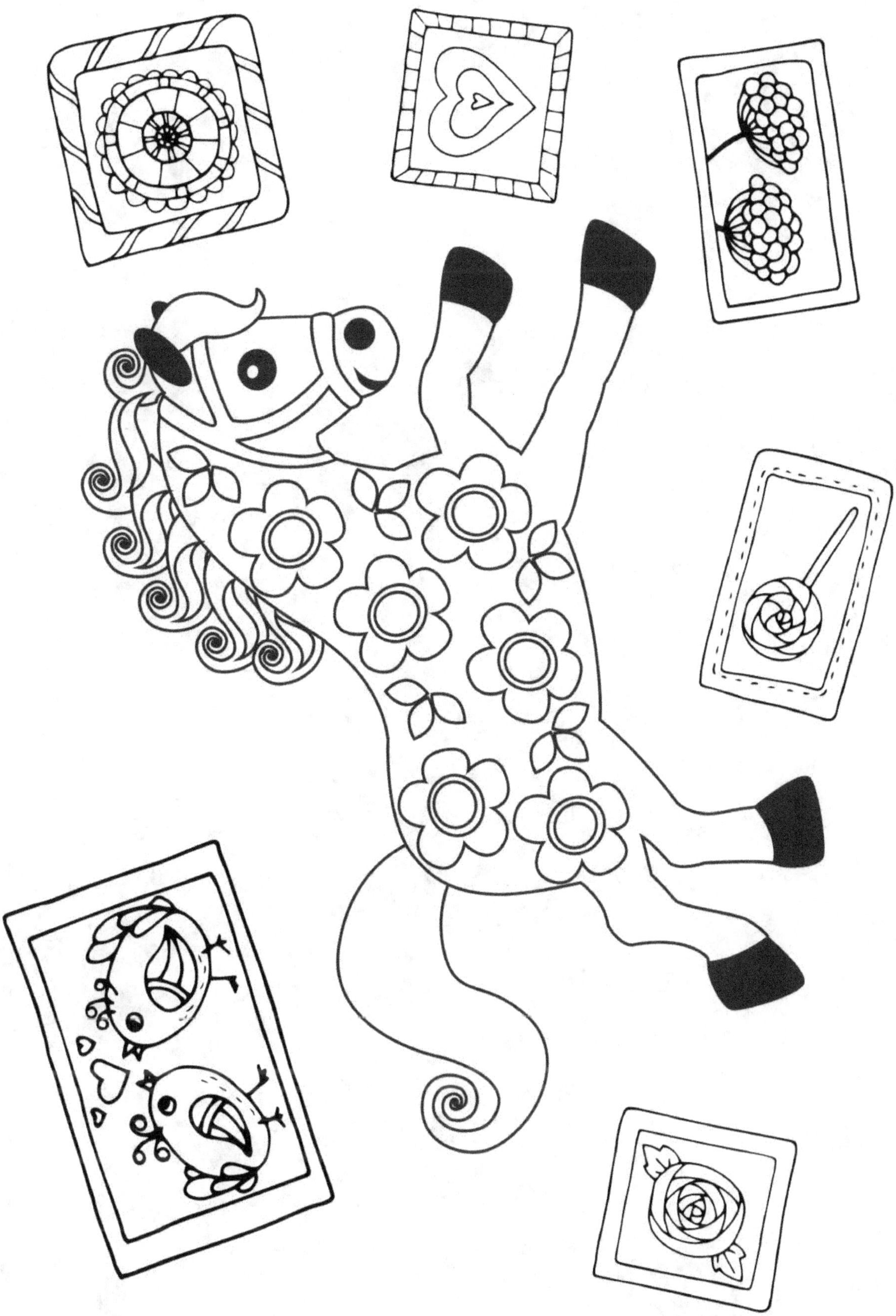

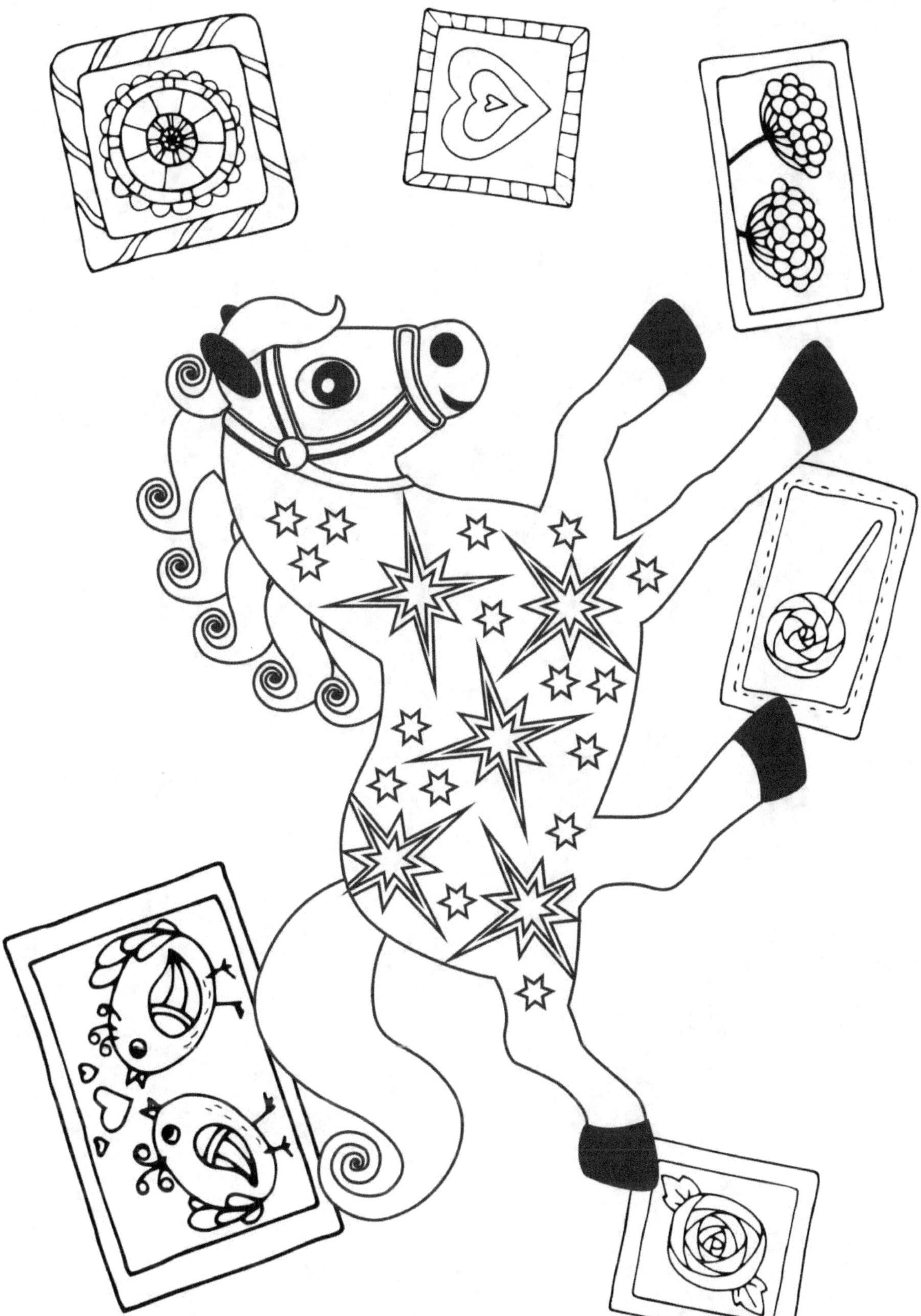

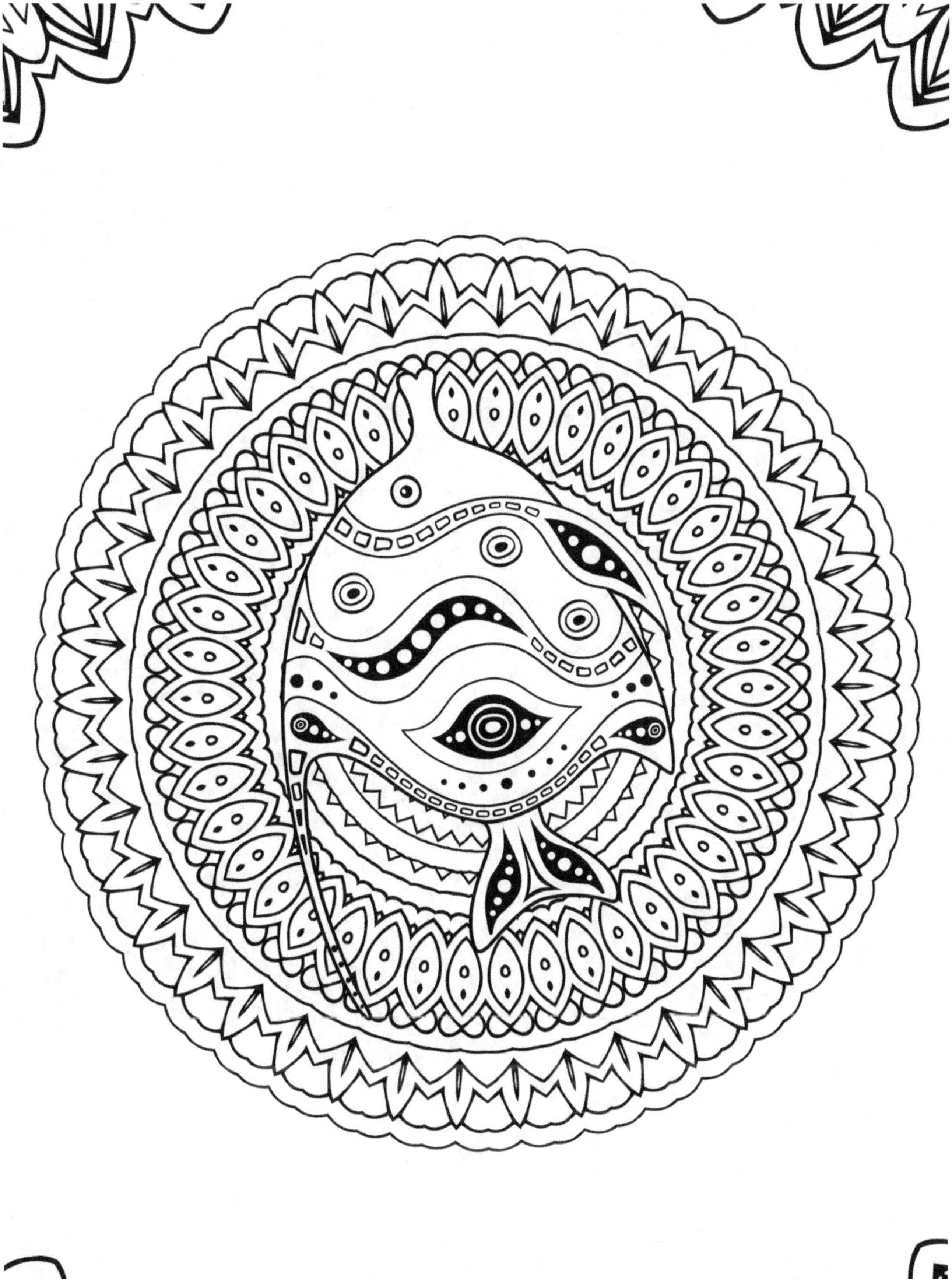

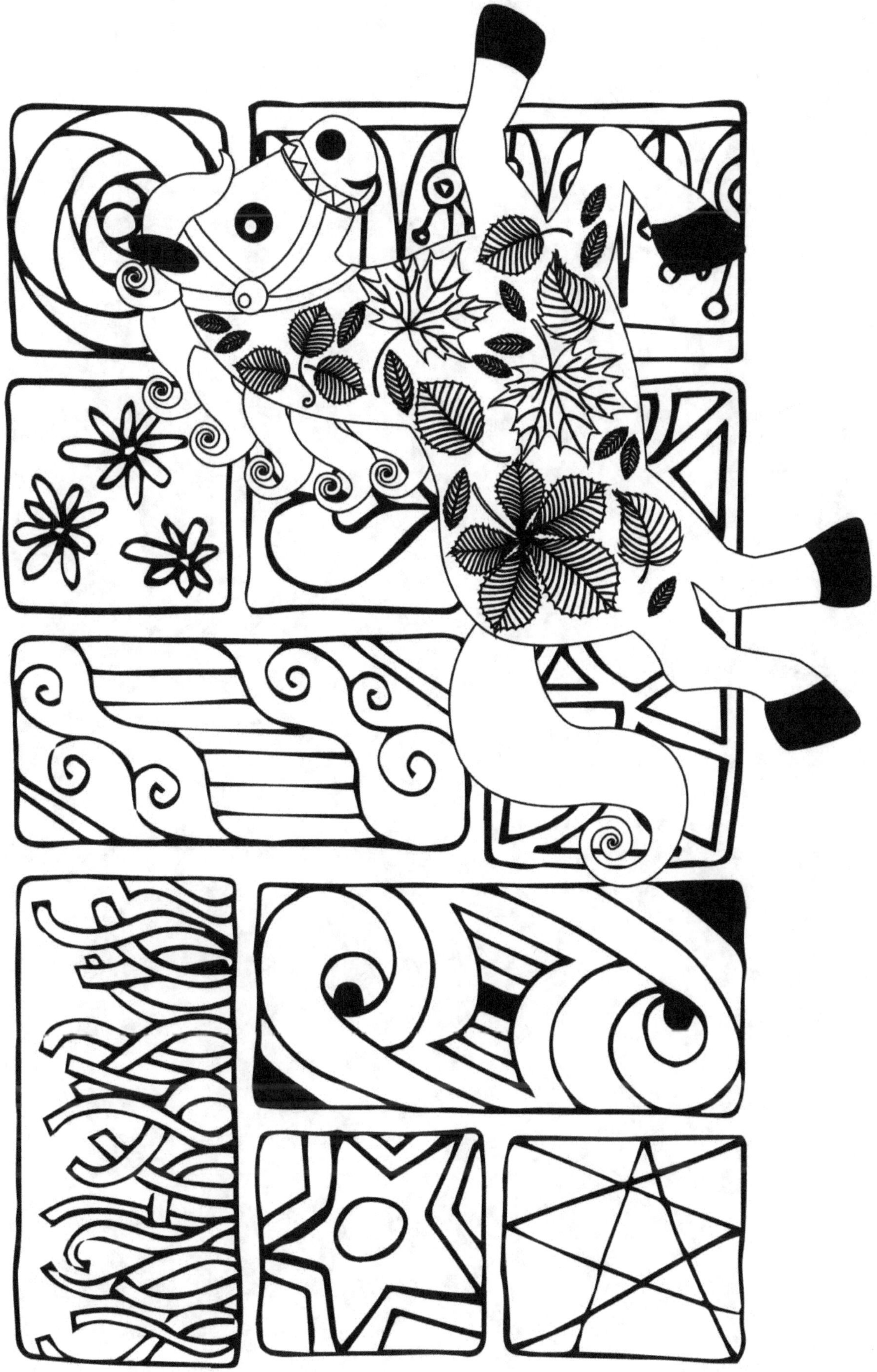

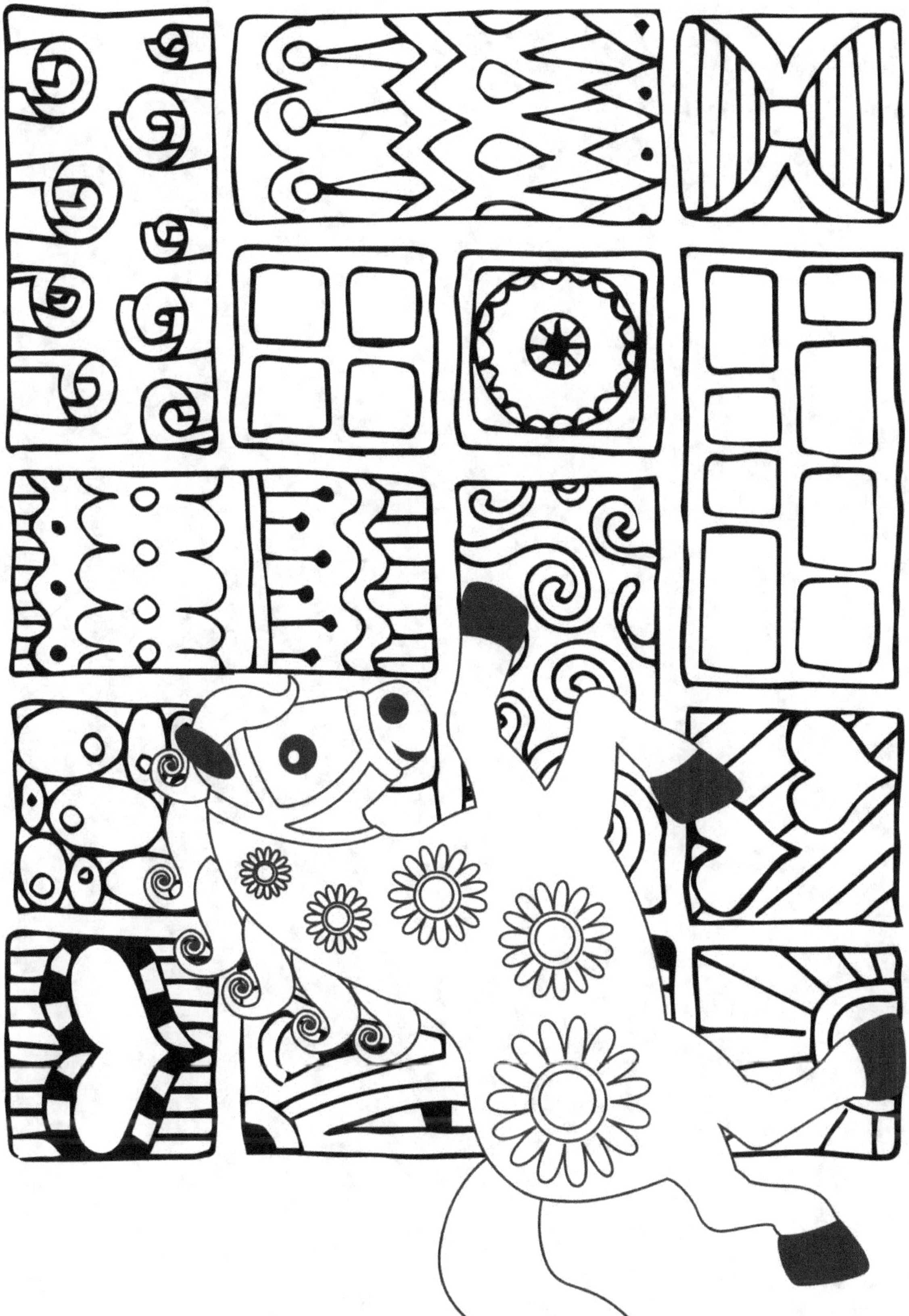

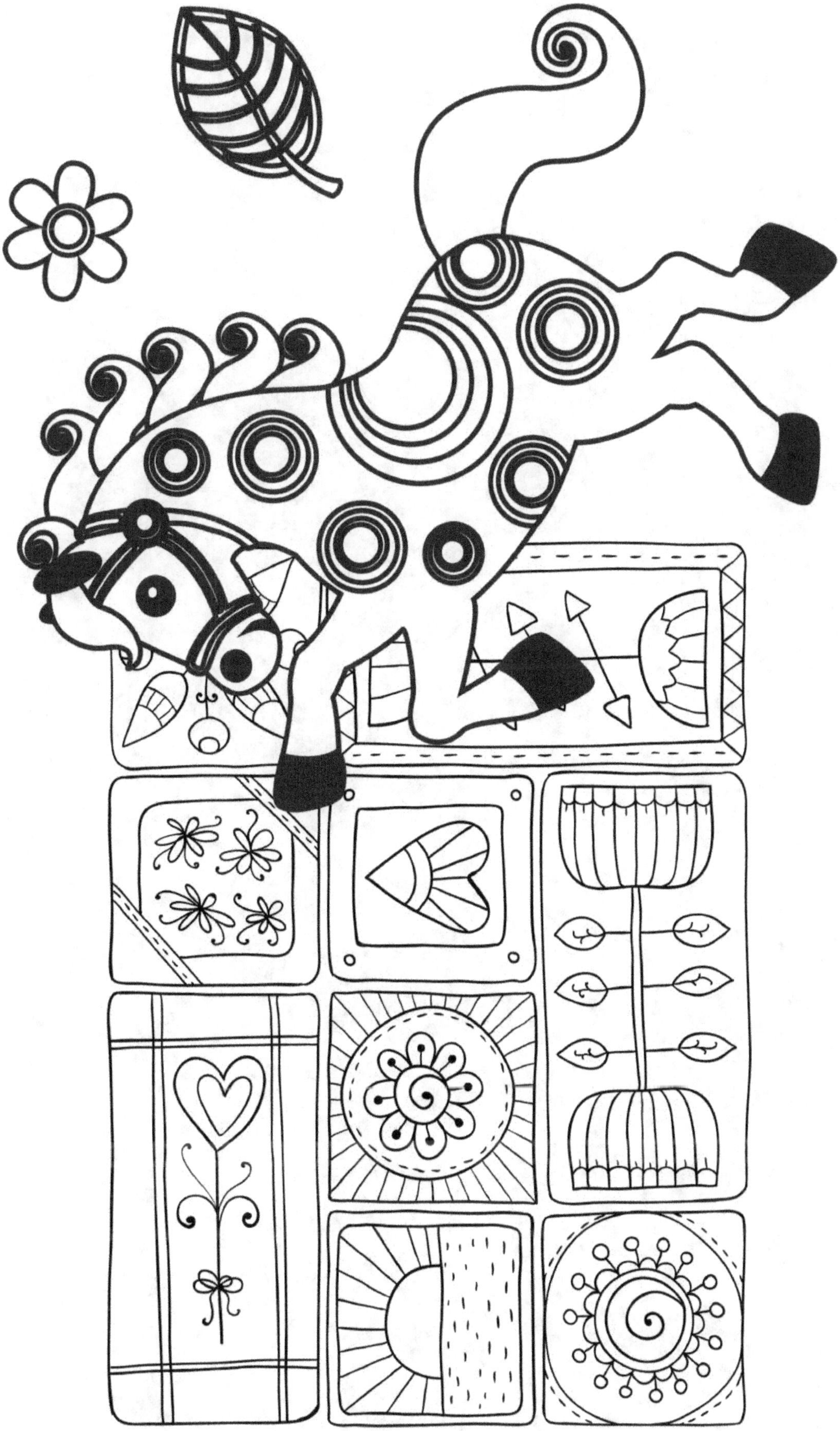

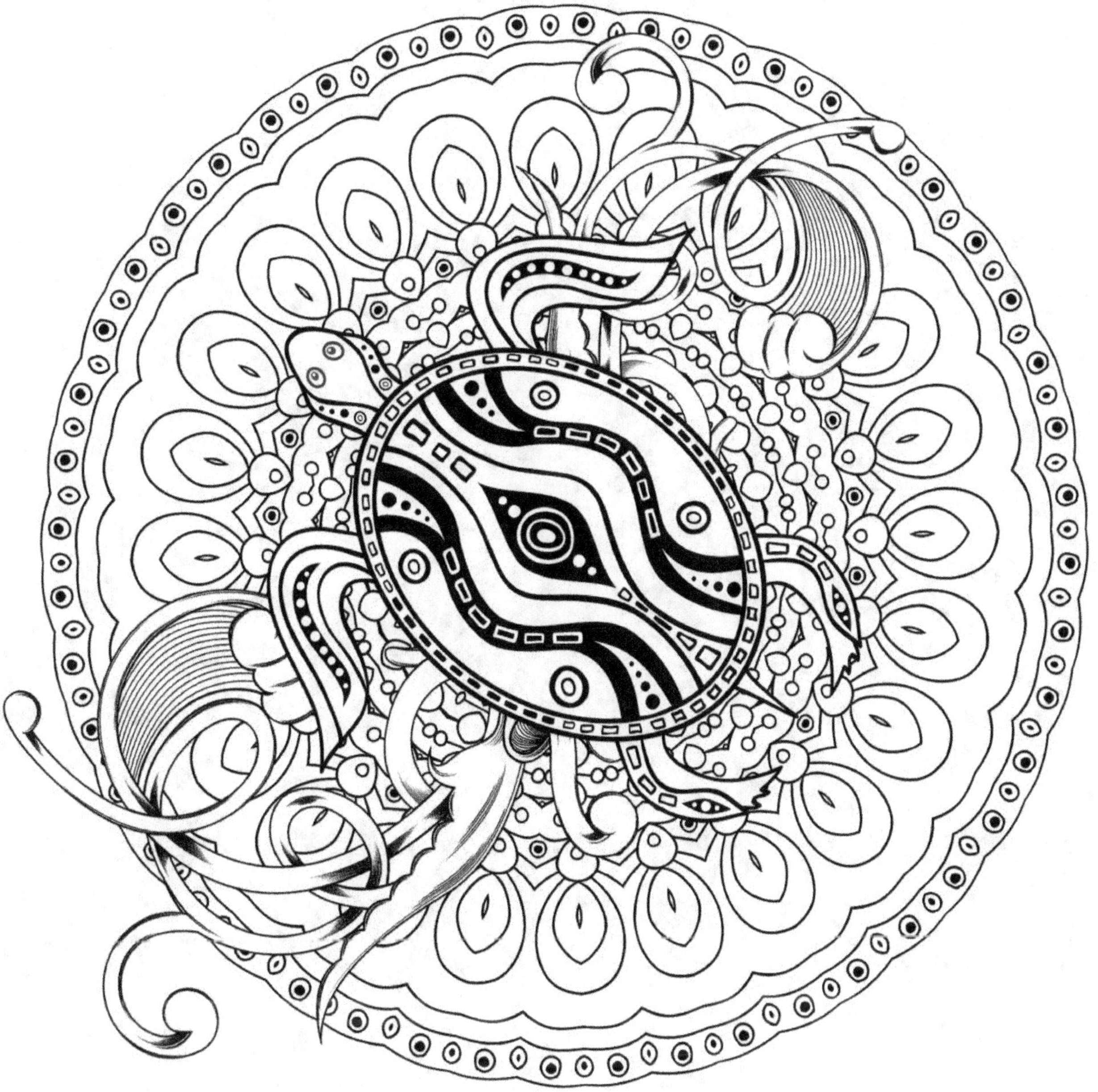

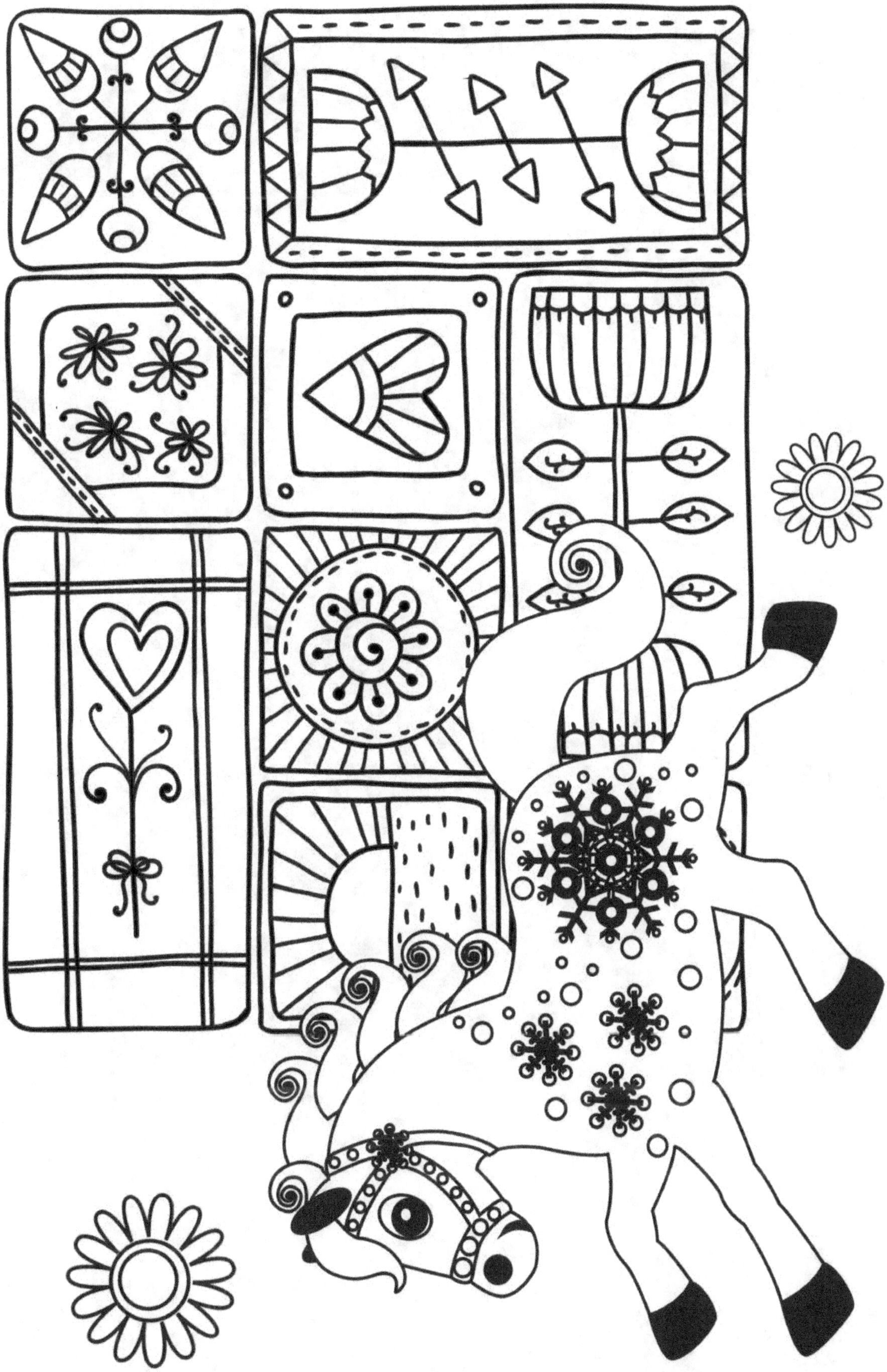

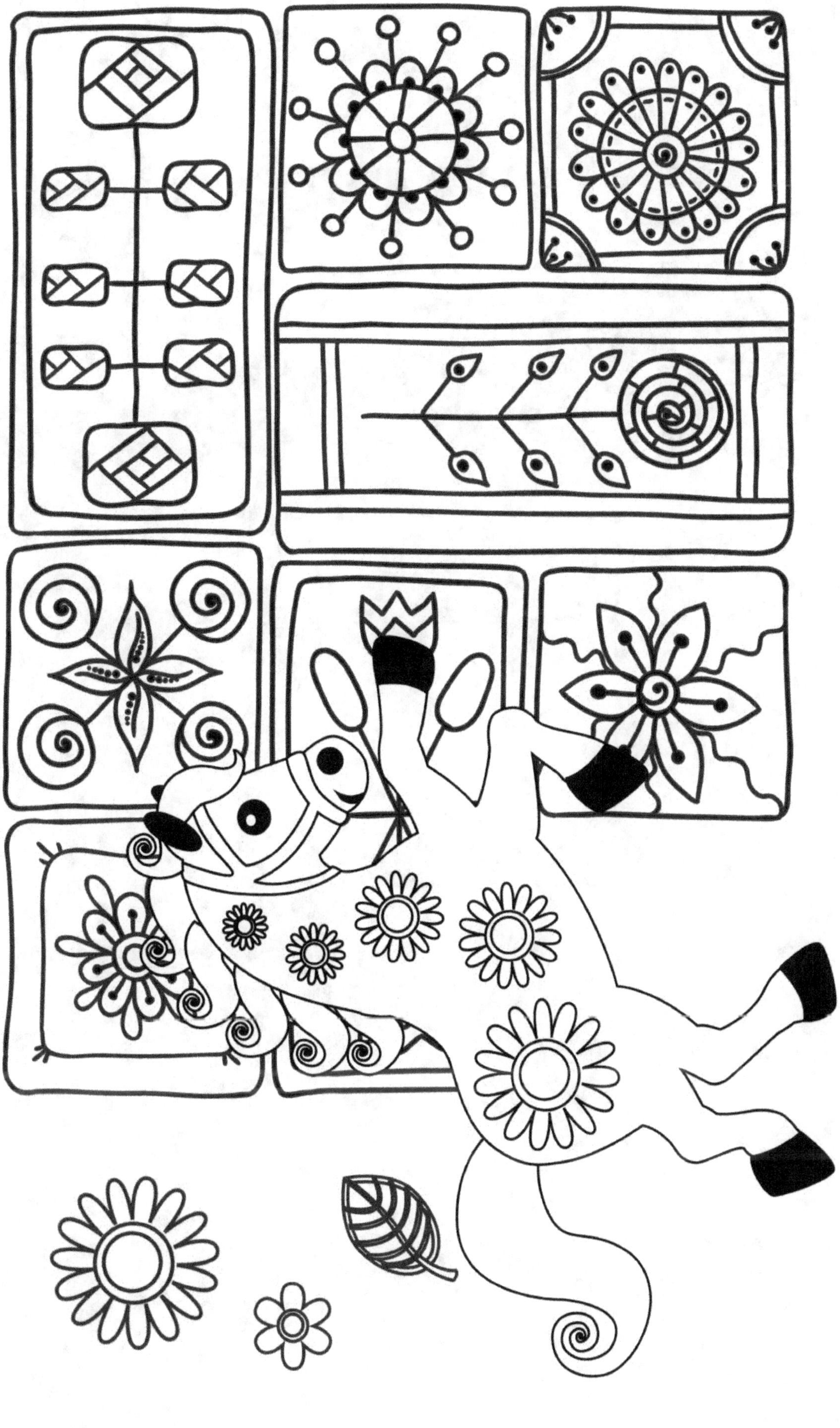

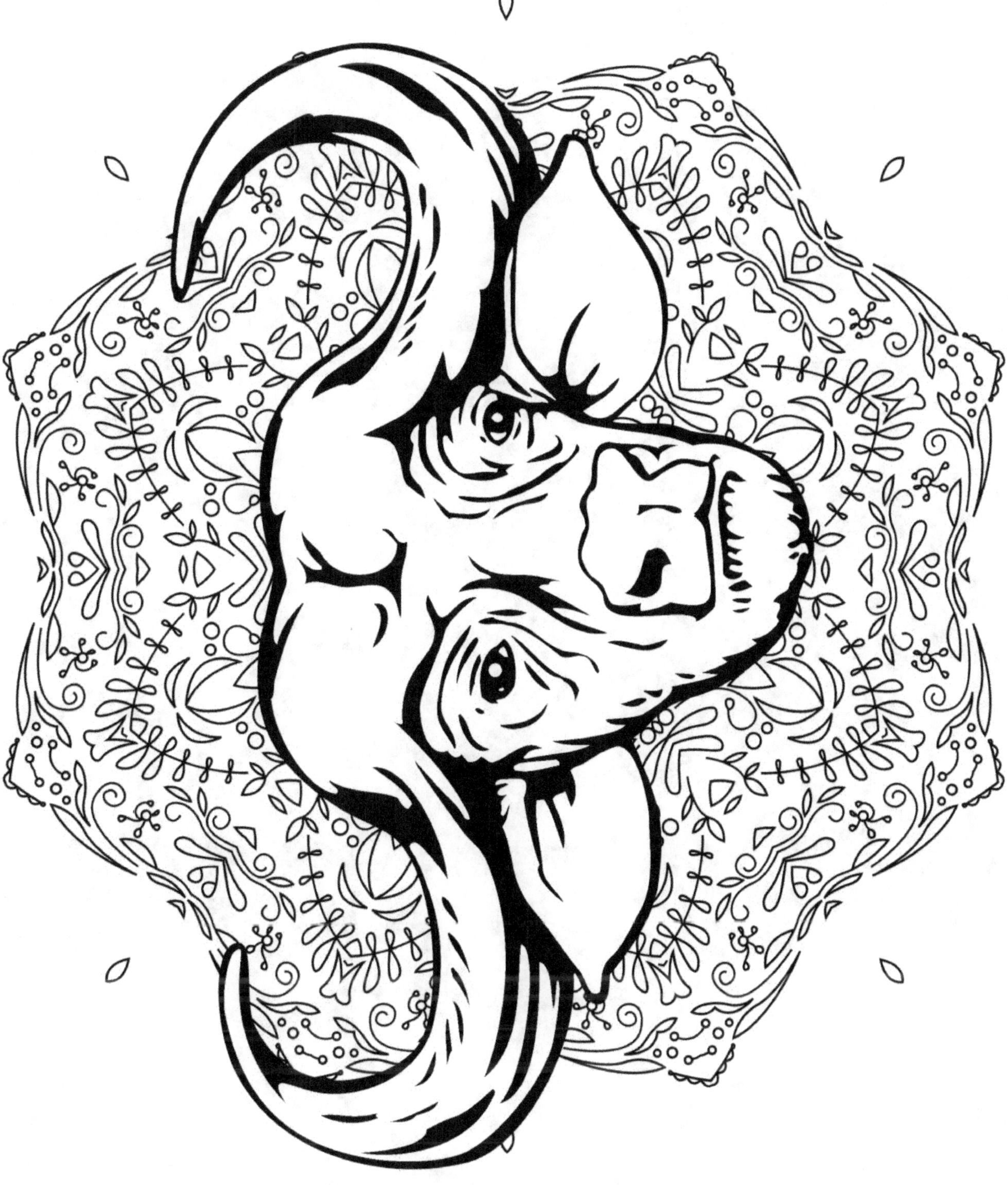

www.ingramcontent.com/pod-product-compliance
Lightning Source LLC
Chambersburg PA
CBHW081214180526
45170CB00006B/2337